MW00323667

Praise For *SHIFT*

SHIFT is a must-read for any individual but, most importantly, every athlete. Athletes have to transition from offense to defense, defense to offense. We have to handle whatever our opponents give us based on our own strategy, all while working in conjunction with teammates and other factors. Like life, we have to shift our focus from wants and needs to purpose and identity. This book forced me to really sit down and ask the tough questions to better understand what my shift will look like for my next transition. Jonathan does a great job being transparent with his own stories and experiences while including familiar, current events and occurrences to make the book a seamless read.

—Amobi Okugo, professional soccer player, *Forbes* 30 Under 30, founder, A Frugal Athlete

Jonathan brings his wealth of knowledge and personal experience working with pro athletes through transition. In *SHIFT*, he takes athletes on a journey of discovery and inspiration that will not only impact their current reality but also prepare them for a successful shift to life beyond their sport.

—Dior Ginyard, *Forbes* 30 Under 30, director, player affairs NFL Players Association

Finally, there is a book which addresses the elephant in the room for so many athletes. Sooner or later, all professional athletes have to retire, and now they have a toolkit to manage this critical transition in the life journey. Jonathan does a brilliant job of turning a major life challenge into an opportunity and self-discovery.

SHIFT is the ultimate playbook to winning where it matters most—life!
—Misha Sher, global head of sport, entertainment, and culture, MediaCom

Jonathan's take on addressing the challenge of what's next in life after the game is powerful. *SHIFT: The Athlete's Playbook* guides athletes through a simple but undervalued concept—the act of sitting down and making time to think about who you are and what you want to do. From the importance of shifting focus, attention, and mindset, coupled with the understanding of who you are through your values, the story you tell yourself and what really matters to you—the process works. Through his own story and experience moving into his next chapter, Jonathan provides a tool to help you unlock the power of self-awareness and the ability to shift your identity as you grow. I recommend this to any athlete who has been thinking about life after the game or any person experiencing a major transition in their lives—an invaluable resource.
—Danielle Berman, founder and CEO, Tackle What's Next

SHIFT is an absolute necessity for any athlete, whether it be starting out or approaching retirement. The correlation between life as an athlete and life in general is explored and challenges the individual to dig deeper to face and prepare for the inevitable transition from sport to life after. A Must Read!
—Nick Addlery, professional soccer player, entrepreneur, investor

A book like this is long overdue! After over forty years coaching in college, it is clear to me that young men and women need help when their athletic career is over. While the graduates are prepared for the workforce or graduate school academically, most are not prepared to give up a sport they have played for many years. Moving from a very competitive sporting environment to a more recreational environment or no sports at all is very difficult. *SHIFT* will guide athletes from the sporting environment to the real world. It is a must-read for all collegiate and professional athletes making the transition to life.

—Dr. Jay Martin, head coach, Ohio Wesleyan University, winningest coach of men's soccer in the NCAA

SHIFT is a must-read for everyone, but all athletes should be required to read this book! As athletes, we often get so caught up in our sport and our identity as an athlete that we lose sight of the other parts of life and the fact that there is a life beyond sport. This book will help guide you through steps to better understand and prepare for those life transitions that are often overlooked. The fact that Jonathan is so transparent about his own experiences adds so much value and relevance and makes this such an enjoyable and worthwhile read.

—Nicole Barnhart, professional soccer player, National Women's Soccer League Players Association Executive Committee

It's a daunting task to try to tackle transition from one point in our life to another. We cannot tackle it alone, and *SHIFT* gives us a template to work through how we are feeling, what our strengths and weaknesses are, and how to come out on the other side thriving and pursuing our passions. I cannot say I have perfected this transition, and I never will, but Jonathan has perfectly paved the road for my personal transition, and I am grateful for his insight. Everyone can take something from this book and be a better person for it.

—Drew Beckie, professional soccer player, entrepreneur

Kary,

Thank you for your continued support and encouragement throughout this journey!

Jonathan Vaitor

SHIFT

The Athlete's Playbook:
5 Proven Steps to Life after Sport

JONATHAN VAN HORN

Published by Author Academy Elite
PO Box 43, Powell, OH 43065
www.AuthorAcademyElite.com

Library of Congress Cataloging: 2021910872

Softcover: 978-1-64746-824-8
Hardcover: 978-1-64746-825-5
E-book: 978-1-64746-826-2

Available in paperback, hardback, e-book, and audiobook

Scriptures marked KJV are taken from the KING JAMES VERSION (KJV): KING JAMES VERSION, public domain.

Scriptures marked ESV are taken from the THE HOLY BIBLE, ENGLISH STANDARD VERSION (ESV): Scriptures taken from THE HOLY BIBLE, ENGLISH STANDARD VERSION ® Copyright© 2001 by Crossway, a publishing ministry of Good News Publishers. Used by permission.

Thank you to my father, who has pushed me to dream bigger than I could have ever imagined and reach higher than I thought was possible.

This book is a testament of your love and investment throughout the years as I wrestled and processed ideas, thoughts, and pushed limits.

Thank you for your encouragement, wisdom, and listening ear!

CONTENTS

INTRODUCTION: THE *SHIFT*   xi

PART 1: START NOW

CHAPTER 1   DO ATHLETES REALLY DIE TWICE?   3
CHAPTER 2   YOUR STORY HAS POWER TO IMPACT
             YOUR WORLD   19
CHAPTER 3   ARE YOU A ONE-TRICK PONY?   30

PART 2: HEART

CHAPTER 4   DISCOVER THE *COR* STRENGTH OF YOUR LIFE   41
CHAPTER 5   UNDERSTANDING THE LENS THROUGH
             WHICH YOU VIEW YOUR LIFE   57
CHAPTER 6   LIFE THEMES: EXPLORING YOUR
             DÉJÀ VU EXPERIENCES   70

PART 3: IMAGINE THE FUTURE

CHAPTER 7 HOW WILL YOU DREAM WITH PURPOSE AND
ACTION? 89

CHAPTER 8 HAVE YOU EVER BUILT A MAP WITHOUT A
DESTINATION? 102

CHAPTER 9 DON'T GO ALONE: HOW BUILDING A TEAM
WILL TAKE YOU FURTHER 111

PART 4: FOCUS

CHAPTER 10 THINKING WITH THE END IN MIND REVISITED 127

CHAPTER 11 CLARIFY WHAT SUCCESS MEANS TO YOU 139

CHAPTER 12 FINDING BALANCE:
THE POWER OF SAYING *NO* AND *YES* 149

PART 5: TAKE ACTION

CHAPTER 13 ROW, ROW, ROW YOUR BOAT! 166

CHAPTER 14 WHAT IS TRULY HOLDING YOU BACK? 178

CHAPTER 15 WHY THE BEST IDEAS COME
TO MIND IN THE SHOWER 193

CONCLUSION: KEEP MOVING AND TAKE THE NEXT BEST STEP 205

ACKNOWLEDGMENTS 211

APPENDICES 213

ABOUT THE AUTHOR 219

BIBLIOGRAPHY 221

INTRODUCTION
THE *SHIFT*

In a time of rapid change, standing still is the
most dangerous course of action. If you don't
learn how to make good transitions, you either
get run over or left behind.

—Brian Tracy

There are few circumstances in which I feel more calm,
at peace, and myself than when I'm engaged in sport and
competition. From a young age, I eagerly anticipated
competing, and all that goes into playing a game, and
I found such joy stepping onto the field or court. I still
can feel the crisp fall air as the wind hit my face, and I
slowed down to gaze at the deep green grass. I can recall
the brightness of the sun bouncing off of the dew on
the morning grass and the sound of the lawnmower as
it cruised past before the game got started. Even today,
when I smell freshly cut grass, those memories and

images of those early years playing the game I love are seared into my mind and always bring a smile to my face.

Football (soccer), basketball, and baseball were my sports, and I loved every minute. Playing gave me joy, life, a place of acceptance, and a place to be myself. What was at first innocent joy and freedom on the face of a child, however, soon began to disappear. I was still accepted and known—at least for what I could do on the field. There was a subtle shift, however, as I grew older, and the stakes began to get higher. This change began with a focus on the results. All eyes were on what I was doing, and competition, the numbers, the winning, and the results started to become my identity.

I realized that through sport, I could be accepted, and people liked me and cheered for me. I could walk into a new environment on a basketball court to play pick-up, and after playing only a game or two, I was accepted and celebrated.

Somewhere along the way, the joy of the game and the freedom that I experienced in those early years began to shift and change to an internal game I was playing against myself—a game in which I kept a close eye on the results, where the score was determined by who I was accepted by, what coach was watching, or the news article online from the local news outlet. When I experienced success and winning, I felt accepted, valued, and significant as a winner!

My sport, my athletic competition, and my performance slowly shifted from what I do to who I am. My value, significance, and my acceptance were determined by how many points I scored, the number of wins in my season, and the amount of success on the diamond.

> **My sport, my athlete competition, and my performance slowly shifted from what I do to what I am.**

I began to lose who I was on the inside and began to settle and strive for what I could do on the outside. I felt less accepted for being myself and more for what I could give to the coach, fans, or my teammates. I carried the weight of performance and the need to validate my value to coaches, friends, media—to whoever was watching and hopefully cheering.

So, there I was, in this tug-of-war, to understand who I was and whether or not I could truly be myself—assuming I still knew who I was. Yet, still in those moments, I experienced sport as a place that felt like home, where I felt the safest; it was what I knew.

Psychologists say that the three most significant transitions anyone can experience in life are the change of location (moving), a change of job, and having a baby. From experience, I can say all three of those changes can cause some crazy around the house, in your mind, and in your life.

As athletes, we experience those types of transitions often. Whether the off-season, change in sport, new season, new team, moving up, trades, starting a family, or retirement, you get the idea. Transition around sport is common, and transition in sport can win or lose games, trophies, and championships.

The year 2011 was crazy for my family and me. We went through all three of those significant life transitions in the span of two months. We had our third daughter, moved multiple states away, and I took a new job. Those transitions rocked my world. I thought I would be okay; however, the experience completely changed my life. It was hard, and more often than not, I was overwhelmed, struggling to stay afloat and attempting to help my wife and family move into this new area and space.

It was in the midst of that where I truly began to realize that while transition is and can be difficult, transitions can also give you significant opportunities. I began to realize that there are certain things I believed that limited me and impacted how I viewed myself and the world around me. I realized there were aspects of my life, goals, relationships, and perspectives that were holding me back from seeing this new change as an opportunity.

Just as in sport, transitions begin to reveal what makes up a team. How a team navigates the various transitions throughout a game can either create significant opportunities or expose weaknesses. The same is true in our non-sport lives. Transitions reveal the true character and thought processes we currently entertain and feed because there is a sense of unknown, a reality that the next step you take is going to be new territory for you and those around you.

In sport, coaches spend hours going over film, strategy, ideas, personnel, and myriad other things to gain an edge and find success on the field of play to get the results they desire. Coaches then pass on their wisdom, understanding, game plan, and strategy to get the positive results individually and collectively as a team.

The same is true in life. The question is whether you have prepared for those transitions. Have you spent the time, energy, money, emotions, and thoughts to have success in and through the transitions in your life and sport? The harsh reality is that even the most successful athletes have a limited time to compete. The window to play at the highest levels is so small. Even those who retire in their thirties still have decades left to live their lives. So, the hard question is will you be ready to make the transition? Even if you only play through university, you will go pro in something other than your sport, and if you have focused your time, money, and energy toward your sport, what will your life look like once your sport can no longer support you?

My hope is that you play your sport for as long as possible, but it will come to an end at some point. Will you be ready? In *SHIFT*, you will go through a five-step framework that will assist you in successfully maximizing your transition. You will look at life transition, and *SHIFT* will be your playbook and provide you with the tools and direction to navigate successfully through the various transitions in sport and life.

S — Start Now
H — Heart
I — Imagine the Future
F — Focus
T — Take Action

This book will help you identify who you are, understand your story, and how to leverage your experience as an athlete and in life. You will clarify your why and understand what is at the core of what drives you and has given you the motivation to be successful in your competition. You will explore and dream about what life after sport could look like and begin to bring into focus that vision so you can live life to the fullest. You will work to understand and remove those limiting beliefs you have acquired along the way and overcome them. Finally, you will work on some of the basic fundamentals as you build upon and form a strong foundation for your life now and wherever your next career transition takes you.

As an athlete, you know or at least have a good idea of what your strengths and abilities are. You know what you bring to the table for the team for which you are playing. But what about in life? What's holding you back, limiting your growth and progress? What are the obstacles preventing you from being victorious? Are you prepared to navigate successfully the significant transitions life will throw at you?

Let me be your coach as you prepare for those moments that will shape your life. In sport, transitions can be what makes or breaks you and your team; and the same can be true in life. I am excited to begin the journey with you as you discover who you are and give you the tools to equip you to navigate successfully the various transitions in sport and life!

PART 1
START NOW

Twenty years from now you will be
more disappointed by the things that you
didn't do than by the ones you did do.

—Mark Twain

In sport, no team or individual simply jumps into the
season and plays games. Long before the first game, athletes go through pre-season, spring training, mini-camps,
voluntary workouts, etc. The club and coaching staff use
this time to prepare for the season. They identify players,
their strengths and weaknesses, develop team chemistry, grow playbook familiarity, move players around
into potential positions, work through the best starting
line-ups, build a season plan, and work toward putting
together the best team possible for that first game.

In Start Now, that is exactly what you are going to
do for your life and current reality; you will develop and
go through your very own pre-season. You are looking

at various aspects of your life and gathering information together to begin establishing a strong foundation to prepare yourself for the life and career you desire moving forward. Over the next few chapters, you will take a deep dive into the three elements of Start Now: Your Identity, Your Story, and Your Experience. These three key elements make up the foundation of your life, your past history, and what has shaped who you are today, and they shed light on the underlying reasons for how and why you respond and act in the present. The more you understand about yourself and grow in your self-awareness, the stronger your life foundation will be moving forward.

It's time to get to work; no more waiting or delaying. The author Stephen King said it well. "Amateurs sit and wait for inspiration, the rest of us just get up and go to work."

You are no amateur. You have worked hard for the success you have achieved as an athlete and in your sport. Now is the time to take that success to the next level within each aspect of your life. Time to *Start Now!*

CHAPTER 1
DO ATHLETES REALLY DIE TWICE?

Plans are useless,
but preparation is indispensable.

—Dwight D. Eisenhower

There is an old adage in athletic circles that athletes die twice—once when they physically die and the other when they finish competing in their sport. The latter is the more difficult to experience. I can relate to this because I felt the emotion and reality when I put on my jersey for the last time. The reality that I was never going to do that again. I was never again going to be on another team, compete at an elite level, or experience everything that comes with team competition. Jokes and banter in the locker room, shared life together, pre-game meals, traveling to away games; it was all over and done, and the final whistle had blown on my athletic career!

This harsh reality didn't fully sink in until a few years later, though, when my life changed significantly. A few years after graduation, I was no longer competing, and fans neither knew my name nor recognized me. While it was on a much smaller scale than those in the professional sports ranks experience, it still feels good when someone you don't know recognizes you. What I began to experience was an emptiness, a gap that hadn't been there before.

I was working with Athletes in Action (AIA) and was doing well in my role. I was married and enjoying life. Yet, there was a sense of loss I would feel at various times, and I didn't know what it was. So, I dismissed what I was feeling, pushed it down. It didn't matter how hard I pushed or how much work, time, and effort I put into my job and marriage; that feeling was still there. I was still around the game and sport here and there, but it was never the same as what I experienced when I was on a team. My reality began to sink in; I was done competing. There would be no more locker rooms, no more playing under the lights. Would that mean no more me?

When asked about the game, professional Belgian Footballer Kevin De Bruyne (who, at the time I write this, is playing with Manchester City in the English Premier League), said, "Weddings, funerals, births? It's nothing. I'm a rock. But if you take football away from me? Forget it. I can't cope."

> "Weddings, funerals, births? It's nothing. I'm a rock. But if you take football away from me? Forget it. I can't cope."
> — Kevin De Bruyne

What De Bruyne and so many other athletes experience and come to believe about themselves is that they are nothing without their sport. Identity, value, and significance are determined by the sport they play and how well they compete. That is why athletes experience two deaths in their life, with the first coming when they stop playing their sport. The first death is the most difficult.

But should we hold fast to this idea that who we are is determined by what we do? Because sport is something we do, and at the professional level, it is a job athletes perform and compete in each and every day. When athletes are done competing, it can feel as if their life is over. In a sense, a death occurs, and athletes go through a very real grieving process.

Why do athletes experience this death? What is it about sport that athletes tie so much of who they are and their significance into a game?

Questions to Ask *before* Your Athletic Career Dies

A few of the more basic and fundamental questions we ask in life are, "Who am I? What is my purpose? What am I living for? Where do I belong?" Sport often answers these elemental questions about our lives. Teams give us a sense of belonging and of being a part of something bigger than ourselves. Sport gives purpose, direction, and structure, the desire to win, achieve high performance, and ultimately find success in championship trophies and rings. From the outside looking in, sport and competition seem to be an important way to define your value and who you are based on your results and performance.

But what happens when you are you longer competing in your sport?

Athletes are accustomed to change. Transitions in sport are some of the most critical moments of competition. Whether it is the fast-break monster dunk in basketball, a turn-over in football, the walk between the green and next tee box for the golfer, the counter-attack in soccer, the handoff in the relay race—the list goes on and on. Those transitions can make or break you as an athlete and as a team.

Entire game plans and strategies are centered around those moments in sport. Transitions reveal and expose whether or not you are prepared for that moment. Athletes and coaches plan, strategize, and prepare for those moments. Those transitional moments can create euphoric celebration or utter defeat.

The same is true for an athlete when they transition into their next phase of life: when their contract ends, and they are no longer competing as a pro, when they graduate from university, or even when they are merely getting older and no longer are able to compete at a high level.

You have given your everything to the sport, coaches, teammates, club, fans and yet as soon as the game no longer needs you, you are cast aside for the next player behind you and left to figure it out on your own. One day you're a teammate, the next, team-less.

So, when the transition to life after sport arrives, will you be ready? Will you be prepared to move into the next arena when the game ends, you get injured, or you experience a global pandemic like we currently are with the coronavirus, and all games, sport, and seasons have been either suspended or canceled? No more numbers, no more stats, no more results. When your sport becomes the only or the main thing that answers these key questions about yourself and life, when the game is gone, the core essence of who you believe you are is also gone.

Are you ready?
Will you be prepared?
How will you navigate this transition?
Change is inevitable!

The important factor for you is to decide whether or not you are going to stay where you are or continue to move forward. The choice is yours though, no coach, teammate, media, or agent can make it for you. Time to take that first step and examine these key questions: What are you living for? Who are you? What's your purpose? Time to take your first step forward as you begin your own pre-season. Let's go!

Don't Buy into the Lies

Questions about life, meaning, value, and significance are answered and developed in various ways. As athletes, most of these questions are answered by our sport and competition. As an athlete, you get sucked into putting your identity and value in your sport and performance. You begin to believe that your purpose and who you are is in direct correlation to how well you perform and the number of wins you tally.

In the 90s, I remember a clothing line with the tag line of "Soccer is life. The rest is just details." They also used football, baseball, volleyball, etc., in the tagline. Many people—myself included—bought into this idea, and maybe you have too. So, let's take a closer look at these lies that culture and sport promise yet fall short of fulfillment of and answering those significant questions about life and sport.

These core questions of who you are, what's your purpose, and what determines your value are either answered intentionally by you or you allow culture to answer them for you. There are three lies that culture and sport shout that are used to create your identity and answer these questions. Realistically, you don't recognize the lies because you love the game and have been playing it for most of your life. You don't even know it is a lie until you begin to explore, examine, and eventually discover the truth.

The three lies that sport and culture use to define, give value, and label you, are:

1. You are what you do.
2. You are what you own.
3. You are what others say about you.

We will examine each of these lies and then replace them with a truth that gives clarity to who you are, your purpose, and your passion.

You have been extremely focused on your job, your craft, your performance, and the results that have culminated in your success. Sport is one of the few vocations that continue to prolong your youth. Soccer, basketball, baseball, etc.—they are all games played by youth who eventually grow up and move onto something else, a *real* job. But when you have the opportunity to play the sport you love and get paid for it, the game turns into something much greater than a job.

This whole idea is fleshed out through one's pursuit to win! Results are a must because, at the end of the day, you've got to win, you've got to produce positive results! If you don't have results, you know you're not winning, and people are going to push you off to the side, forget you, and reinforce that small voice inside saying you are not good enough. Again, the lie rears its ugly head.

If you don't produce, if you don't put a strong product out on the field, court, or pitch, and the results don't meet expectations, then you are no longer of value or needed. So, you get cut, released, or don't get a contract extension or renewal—and that's hard! It's mentally taxing, and so we take that same idea, that same results-driven focus and put it into ourselves. If I don't perform well, then I have no value, no significance.

When your identity is associated with your sport, your performance, or the lack thereof, directly correlates in your mind to who you are. You define yourself through the lens of your performance, wins and losses, and data analytics.

Internalizing that you are not what you do is one of the hardest obstacles to overcome. You are not defined by your sport and your performance, yet as an athlete and team, that is how you are measured every day. Your performance—goals scored, stats, minutes, contracts—they are all measured, analyzed, and critiqued, and then you are given a value within the sport culture based on that data. There are even websites that assign a value to professional soccer players from around the world, determining or estimating the player's worth based on performance.[1]

As athletes, we don't even realize we have bought into the lie. When I was in sixth grade, the first time I experienced the power and influence I had as an athlete and how others viewed and valued me based on my abilities and athletic talents was on the playground.

It was my first day at a new school, and we all went out for recess. The captains were picking teams, and after I was picked, someone asked about being quarterback. I jumped in and said, "I can throw."

Whether the other kids were being nice because I was new, they said okay. On the first play, I threw a bomb for a touchdown. Everyone came running back to me, giving me hugs and high-fives. From that day forward, I was the first pick at recess.

What I took from that day was that if I played well and won, people would like me and view me as valuable. But what I also learned that day was if I didn't play well and win, then people would not like me. So, I worked hard to make sure I won and that people would like me; I began to see myself as the athlete—the winner!

What started that day in sixth grade continued on for many years after. My life was a roller coaster of emotions and mental fortitude filled with ups and downs at every practice, training, and every game. When my play decreased, so did my value and significance. I thought less of myself because my performance was poor. The opposite was true; when I played well and performed at a high level, I had a high value to those around me and in my own eyes.

But the roller coaster got old quickly and the weight to perform at a high level was heavy on my soul, mind, and body, but I pushed forward because I believed the lie.

As an elite athlete, you are given the opportunity to play a game and even get paid. Then, seemingly out of nowhere, harsh reality hits, and it's gone—your career is over, and you are left with nothing. Not only is your sport over, but so is your life. Well, at least that is the lie you have been told and what it feels like in that moment.

The second lie you are told is that you are what you own, and this lie goes beyond the sport culture. Your value is seen and determined based on the house you live in, the vehicle you drive, the clothes you wear, and the accessories you carry. The fancier, more luxurious or limited edition *things* you own, the more valuable you are to the world. There is a pull in our hearts' desire that we crave to been seen, to be noticed, to be known. So, the lie promises to fulfill your desire to be seen based upon what you own.

You work harder, train longer, and are more focused on your performance and sport, so you have the money and opportunity to own more things. The lie is that when you own more, you will have more value, meaning, and significance to offer the world around you.

The problem with this lie is that you can never own enough. It is like pouring water into the sand on the beach; as soon as the water touches the sand, it is gone, no matter how much water you pour. The water is gone, and shortly thereafter, even the wet surface sand dries out, and there is no evidence water was even there. The Roman stoic Seneca stated, "It is not the man who has too little, but the man who craves more, that is poor."

We have been told the lie that the more we have, the better we will feel about ourselves and the more value we will have in society and to others, but with each purchase, you are left wanting more. Even what you have eventually becomes unimportant or valueless to you and others.

The third lie has become more and more influential in the past decade with the rise and emphasis on analytics and data. Athletes are now critiqued and scrutinized in more ways and in more detail than ever before. Technology writer Andrew Wooden wrote, "Sport is evolving. In future athletic competitions, gold medals won't just be won on the track; they'll be won in the data centre."[2] Wooden continues, "As analytical programs become more sophisticated, improved algorithms will be able to convert data into more sophisticated insights to help athletes maximize their performance." As more data is used to help athletes improve, that same data will also be used to scrutinize an athlete's performance.

Now, don't get me wrong, I think the rise in data analytics is growing the game. Athletes are getting better, faster, and stronger as more data is used and utilized.

The negative side effect is that athletes are now, more than ever, analyzed with a fine-tooth comb! That not only adds pressure to perform at a high level but also contributes to the struggle with not buying into the lie that you are what others say about you. Whether you are labeled as an athlete, a success, or a failure, the weight of those lies is real and heavy to carry. By taking the words of others and using them to define who you are, your view of self can change in an instant. So, if we believe what is being said about you, your perspective and view of yourself will also ebb and flow with the perspectives of other people.

So how do you overcome these lies from sport, the athletic world, your performance, and a culture that have been used to define you? What are the steps you can take to reject the lies and grab hold of truth and live out your authentic self?

Three Keys to Developing a Healthy Identity and Self-Awareness

1.   Clarify your standard — your ideal, best character.

As humans, we are not designed to develop our identity from our job, vocation, or what we do, but rather, we reflect identity through our behaviors, choices, and character. When we get this backwards, we create confusion, disorder, and a delusional perspective of self, because jobs—whether we are playing a game or work in a marketing firm—are the avenue by which our identity is expressed through our character and choices. The job title or job itself, however, is not what we use to define who we are or the essence of our humanity.

Living toward the *Standard* gives a direction or north star for you to strive to be at your best. Therefore, clarifying what your best looks like and how it is actioned out in and through your life gives focus to your identity. Moreover, the simple practice of visualization helps refine what your best self looks like in action and helps provide a framework to live out those actions.

What does the *Standard* look like for you? Do you want to have a standard to win at all costs? Or would you rather reflect grit, determination, focus, and intentionality? When you highlight results, wins and losses or stats, you fall back into the trap that what you do is who you are, and your identity is defined by your sport or job. Your vocation is used to reflect your identity, not the medium used to define your identity. You change your perspective to getting better every day, and striving toward the *Standard*.

2. Know your core beliefs.

All of the three keys are intertwined and connected. When you compromise on one, you are removing, eliminating, or affecting part of the other two keys. If I take my identity from what I do, then you are willing to compromise your beliefs for the sake of the result (the win) needed to validate self-worth and significance. When recognizing all three keys as fully interconnected, you cannot remove or compromise on one without affecting all three aspects of identity formation, just as you can't take one wheel away from a tricycle and still expect it to work well. You may still move, and even in the direction you desire to go, but it will not work or function the way it is designed.

Core beliefs give clarity to what the standard looks like through actions and character. Values and beliefs are reflected through character and lifestyle. We will take a deep dive into clarifying your personal values later in the book, but for now, let's focus on core beliefs.

Your core beliefs are the truths that you espouse deep down and the perspectives you carry that you are not willing to jeopardize in thought or action.

Core beliefs are the ideals that you bring to the table that make up your reality and the space around you. They are the basic point of view you have about yourself, other people, and the world. Your core beliefs are the truths that you espouse deep down and the perspectives you carry that you are not willing to jeopardize in thought or action. Your core beliefs are developed through personal faith, one's religious or family traditions, or personal experience from your past that has resulted in your present view that guides or directs your life.

I want to acknowledge now that we all have some beliefs in our lives that do hold us back or limit us. In the *Take Action* step, we will take a closer look at limiting beliefs and how they negatively affect your mindset and perspective. I will guide you step by step on how to create a plan to identify those limiting beliefs, reject them, and replace them with positive truths about yourself.

In this chapter, let's focus on the positive core beliefs that you desire to hold onto and use to build upon in your life. So, how do you identify these core beliefs? To have a healthy identity, we need to have clarity on what creates the healthy identity, and one key aspect is knowing our core beliefs.

Recently I was watching a show about ancient Egypt with my daughter. It was about pharaohs, rulers, mummification practices, and burial tombs from thousands of years ago. In the tombs, they would place treasures plated with gold and other precious metals and artifacts.

One question asked in the documentary was about where the Egyptians found all of this gold. While we were watching, the archeologists shared about digging deep into mountains, searching for veins of quartz, gold, and other precious metals. My daughter asked, "Why do they have to dig so far down into the mountain?"

I responded, "That's where the gold is located. If it was close to the surface, anyone could get it and take it.". [3]

Well, in life, our core beliefs are similar. They are deep down in our subconscious and are usually formed and developed early in our lives. As humans, we need to take the time to dig to discover our core beliefs. This is accomplished by asking curious, thought-provoking, and powerful questions.

When we experience an event, we go through a quick subconscious process: See or Hear the event, Tell ourselves a story from our past, Feel an emotion, and Take Action.

The sequence we go through stems from our core beliefs. To get to the root of your core beliefs, you need to ask a series of questions to help you dig down into the mountain and discover the precious core beliefs like the ancient Egyptians dug deep for the precious metals. When you experience an event or moment, stop and evaluate your response by asking yourself this series of questions.

- What thought came to mind when you experienced _____?
- What did I tell myself?
- Is it true? Is it positive or negative?
- Repeat this question over and over until you believe you have hit your core belief.

- What emotion did I feel?
- Was it positive or negative?
- What does this mean for me?
- Ask the *AWE* question—And What Else?
- Is that true?
- Repeat these previous two questions until you hit your core belief.

Once you discover your core beliefs, you take hold of the positive beliefs and recognize the negative or limiting beliefs (again, we will take a closer look at limiting beliefs later in the book and learn how to replace them with positive beliefs). Your core beliefs are the foundation that you build upon for your identity, and for you to live out the Standard you are pursuing and desiring to live.

3. Build a strong team.

All successful athletes achieved their success with the help and assistance of others: parents, grandparents, coaches, teammates, and sponsors. No athlete achieved success on their own, and the same is true in life. Frankly, I believe we were designed to interact and intentionally engage with others. We were not meant to be isolated; we are meant to live in communities.

Historically, one's identity was cultivated through community—where you grew up, family, extended family, neighborhoods, town, etc. With the development of youth sport in the US and around the world, now more than ever, youth are leaving their local communities to compete and look for new opportunities to play at higher levels or create better opportunities to get recognized for their play.

That fosters an environment where the sport you play begins to be the constant for an athlete as they grow and develop. In those key years, when our identity is being established, it is marked by change and new arenas and spaces. Therefore, creating an identity in athletes leads them to focus on the sport they play rather than the people they are around because their coaches, teammates, and support staff can change from season to season.

Even though you may have limited ability to choose who your community is while growing up, as an adult, you have the ability to choose and build your *team*. You truly are the average of those you spend the most time with and are closest to in life. Your identity is cultivated within that collection of people. It is where you have the ability to change, adjust, and affect your identity based on who you choose to bring into your life.

A good coach sees in you what you don't yet see as an athlete. You want people around you who can see you at your best and encourage you to strive toward and live in that space regardless of the environment. The beauty of your personal *team* is that you also have the opportunity to build and encourage those on your *team*. Booker T. Washington said, "A sure way for one to lift himself up is by helping to lift someone else." You become stronger, better, and healthier through the *team* you are embedded in, and it is a two-way street. As you are being built into by others, you also build into them and collectively, as a *team*, you move toward living, working, competing, and being your best.

The three keys to developing a healthy identity and self-awareness:

1. Striving toward the *Standard* (ideal self, best character).

2. Knowing your positive core beliefs and values.
3. Building a strong team around you.

For athletes, the reality of change is lurking around every corner. Whether you are a professional, university, or even a high school athlete, your career and time competing are eventually going to end. You have poured your life into the sport, and then it is over. That ending creates a massive gap in your life, and there isn't anything else that you want to fill it. It is a void calling out to be filled to make you whole again. It feels as if a piece of who you are is gone, done, and no longer part of your life. And that is why athletes die two deaths.

So, what does this transition that every athlete goes through look like for you? How will you navigate this *death* and significant change in your life? The first step is to develop a healthy identity and grow in your self-awareness as you recognize and reject the three lies that sport and culture tell you every day. To overcome the lies you have been told, start your very own pre-season by creating, clarifying, and establishing a healthy identity and increase your self-awareness!

CHAPTER 2

YOUR STORY HAS POWER TO IMPACT YOUR WORLD

*There's no greater agony than bearing
an untold story inside of you.*

—Maya Angelou

As a culture, we are riveted by a good story. Recently, I have been engrossed in the ESPN 30 for 30 film, *Lance*. The film is the story of Lance Armstrong, his rise to cycling god-like status, and his impending fall from glory due to doping and the use of performance-enhancing drugs. It was amazingly produced and forced you to wrestle with your own ethics and behavior, question your decisions, or wonder why Armstrong made the choices he did. Toward the end of the documentary, Armstrong was asked if he could go back, would he do it all over again, and without hesitation, he said he absolutely would. It was a sobering reality about the choices he had made, but also the power of our stories and how they impact others.

Stories have heroes, tragedies, successes, struggles, wrestling with ethical decisions, pain and suffering, dilemmas, and guides, and they are entertaining because so often you can see parts of your life in the stories of others. You know when you have heard, read, or seen an amazing story; it grabs you and transports you into that moment, and you experience the emotion.

The power of story is there, but one thing you may not know is that your story has all of those same elements I mentioned above. Your story has power and needs to be shared! Your life experience has shaped who you are—your character, your perspective, triggers, thought patterns, emotions, and filters—but the reality is that you probably have not taken the time to remember your story and the elements and experiences that have shaped your life. You have remembered a few significant events that you might say have shaped who you are, but much of your life has been pushed to the back burner of your mind. The memories and experiences are still there, just covered up a bit, like an old desk sitting in an attic covered in dust. Your memories are there; you just haven't thought about them in a long time.

What's Your Story

Stories are powerful and can have tremendous impact on your life. Think about the stories of the great athletes of our generation, those you have watched, wanted to emulate, or were inspired by their story. I can't tell you how many times I have heard that Michael Jordan was cut from his high school team and how that event influenced his life and basketball career, and how those failures and struggles shaped how he competed and drove his passion and intensity on and off the court. In the ESPN production, *The Last Dance*, viewers get an inside perspective of who Jordan was growing up in North Carolina, at the University of North Carolina, with the Chicago Bulls, and during his NBA career, to present day. There were moments in time, events, interactions, and challenges that shaped Jordan's mindset, perspective, attitude, and how he competed. What was amazing was how those moments continue to fuel him day to day.

One aspect I truly enjoyed about *The Last Dance* was the story and the different characters within the story and how the directors intertwined the storylines. Dennis Rodman, Steve Kerr, and Scottie Pippin; each of them had powerful stories and how their stories intertwined with Michael Jordan's story.

Knowing your story is important, but it doesn't stand alone. Your story exponentially grows and increases its impact when you understand and recognize that your story is part of a larger narrative. Your life is not only about you! Your life and story fit into a greater narrative being written all around you. There is an image in the last episode of *The Last Dance* that brings this idea to life. Jordan is speaking after the Chicago Bulls won their sixth NBA Championship in eight years in a packed Grant Park, in the historic Chicago Park District. There are thousands of cheering fans yelling, crying, and celebrating along with Jordan and his team. Jordan shares that his heart, soul, and life are in and part of Chicago, and he is right. People see their lives and story through the narrative of Jordan and his success with the Bulls. Celebrities, icons of Chicago, and others throughout the ten episodes shared their *where they were* moments throughout Jordan's significant moments of his career.

Now, you may never have the impact and influence of Michael Jordan, but there are people in your life who look to you, as many others looked at Jordan. Your story is intertwined with their stories.

Your story is filled with events that have molded you into the athlete you are today. More importantly, those events have shaped the person you are today. Your humanity and what makes you unique is directly correlated to the events, environments, and trauma you have experienced over your lifetime. The power of your story comes from remembering it, sharing it, and understanding how it influences those around you.

The power of your story comes from remembering it, sharing it, and understanding how it influences those around you.

So why don't we truly know our story? Why is it that when asked about who we are, the general response is a list of accomplishments and results? What is the reason for not remembering the various life events and moments that have shaped you?

Your story has power, not because of wins or losses or the number of goals you have scored or the records you have broken or even the sport that you play. No, your story has power because of the character your life has created—the obstacles you have faced and how you responded in those moments, how you have found success and your attitude and actions within those accomplishments, the trouble you have gotten yourself into, the daily choices you have made to create habits, the help you have needed, and those who have come alongside you in those moments to lift you up and encourage you.

As you look to take this first step in your journey, understanding and knowing your story will give you the confidence, whether you are finding success or struggling through failure. Knowing your story will give you a foundation to build upon and reflect upon, knowing where you have come from and all you have learned along the way.

So how do you know, understand, and communicate your story? How do you not simply give the highlight reel from athletic accolades, trophies, and championships, but truly share and communicate the moments, relationships, and events that have shaped who you are today?

Start with the Highlights

When I was growing up in the 1980s, very few people had access to cell phones. There were no apps like Google or Apple Maps or even GPS navigators. We used paper maps purchased from a gas station or an atlas from the local AAA. The maps were folded nice and neat—at least until you unfolded them. Once you flattened out a map, it was almost impossible to refold it the correct way. So, you ended up with a wrinkled, weirdly folded giant piece of paper. I still harbor some frustration from those early years of traveling.

I remember holding this massive atlas on my lap as my family drove across the US from Michigan to visit my grandparents in Arizona. I had the atlas as well as individual maps for each of the states we would drive through. In the atlas, each page consisted of a state or part of a state, depending on the size of the state. There was so much detail, and information about the types of roads, names, state routes, cities, state and national parks, and even other special destination locations, but all of these maps and the atlas was of little value unless I had a destination in mind. On the long trip to Phoenix,

Arizona (over thirty-six hours of driving!), I had each state dog-eared in the atlas, and I highlighted the route we wanted to take to make sure we stayed on track.

Nowadays, you put the address in your cell phone or GPS, and a highlighted route is illuminated for you. No more maps and the pain of attempting to refold them, or a large atlas with all fifty states inside. What's even better is you have a voice to remind you when to turn, tell you what road is coming up, and when you will arrive at your destination. You even have the choice on the type of voice that will speak to you; my daughter loves the female British voice.

Well, your story is like the GPS map. Events, choices, attitudes, and circumstances you have experienced over the course of your time here on Earth are the *highlights* of your life. Winston Churchill said, "The farther backward you can look, the farther forward you can see." Your story carries power and impact—not only for you but also for those in your world. Remember, your story is woven into the stories of others, a larger narrative being written by humanity.

Mile Markers to Watch For

So, how do you intentionally look farther back and remember your story in a way you can intentionally share it with others for your benefit and to build into and inspire others?

Here are six mile markers (prompts) to help you remember, reflect, build, and share your story so you can learn from it and have the opportunity to communicate it with others.

Hero—Joseph Campbell defined a hero as "someone who has given his or her life to something bigger than oneself." Who is a hero for you? People who have intentionally laid down their own interests and have fought for your best interests. Heroes build into the lives of others, knowing that they themselves may never be recognized for their actions or investments. They champion, celebrate, and lift you up, so you have all that is needed to accomplish your hopes and dreams and to live fully.

So, who is your hero(es)? Remember who that is and the reason they are your hero. Their actions, mindset, and fortitude have shaped and molded who you are today. As you put your story together, remember that our heroes are people who inspire us, push us to be better versions of ourselves, and paint a picture of what the future could hold.

History—We are not raised alone, but surrounded by a community early in our lives. Some people are there to help; from others, we experience hurt, but it is with those around us that your identity is cultivated. Your history is the foundation of who you are and how you view yourself. Reflect on your childhood; what stands out, what shaped your ideas, thoughts, and perspectives? What were some family traditions, cultural traditions, or experiences that made you, well you? Whether there was joy, struggle, excitement, change, security, stability, or chaos, your personal history has value and is important to remember and share.

Helping Hand—As athletes and people, we didn't arrive where we are today without the help of another. Marcus Tullius Cicero said that "Not for ourselves alone are we born." Whether it was surviving a deep valley or vicious storm, someone came alongside to protect, encourage, inspire, or build into you during those moments.

We are inspired to help others. Having the experience and opportunity to compete at the elite level of athletics was a result of someone else's investment in your life. Who came alongside you and aided in your development and growth or rescued you from something? How did their investment in your life affect you, your perspective, and how you live your life and compete as an athlete? Whose shoulders are you standing on as you strive toward greatness, success, and being at your best? Part of your story is knowing who has helped you, celebrating them, and understanding what you learned and experienced from that time in your life.

Heartache or Hurt—How have you been hurt by someone else? How has pain, suffering, or trauma influenced your thought, mentality, and character? How has your response to heartache shaped who you are today? Pain, suffering, obstacles are part of life that everyone experience and they reveal your inner resilience, self-confidence, courage, and innovation. People are often shaped more significantly by the hurt, pain, and struggles experienced, than the success.

Whether the hurt is in front of thousands of fans in a stadium or the pain of abuse in your living room, those memories shape the fabric of who we are, and they are yearning to escape and be shared. Your story transcends the souls of others, but only if it is remembered and shared. This area of memories is one of the more difficult to dive into because of the pain and trauma we experience as a result of heartache and hurt, but it is also the most powerful when shared!

Hope—Hope, or the idea of hope, can move people to overcome obstacles, grind through the valleys, and sing from the mountain tops. Hope is a powerful expression and also a simple one. There is one side of hope where you envision a child waiting, hopeful, as she stares at the gifts under the Christmas tree dreaming about that new basketball, glove, or whatever was on her Christmas list. It is like a wishful desire for something.

Then there's a young athlete who pushes through long workouts and trainings while no one is watching, hoping for a better future and the opportunity to compete at the highest level. Will it pay off, will the work go unnoticed, or will all of this work pay off at some point? Franklin D. Roosevelt said, "We have always held to the hope, the belief, the conviction that there is a better life, a better world, beyond the horizon." Hope is what gives you a sense of possibility, a desire that comes to life, and a vision of what your future reality could be!

Regardless of your view of hope, I am going to define it as *a feeling of expectation and desire for a certain thing to happen.* Looking through the filter of hope, who or what brings you hope? I will leave you with this quote from Desmond Tutu to challenge and encourage you. "Hope is being able to see that there is light despite all of the darkness." Where and in what is your hope?

Highlights—What have been the major moments in your life athletically, relationally, educationally, emotionally, and spiritually? What are those shining moments that have been etched in your memory and you are proud of accomplishing? What emotions did you feel, what was the environment like, where were you, who was there, what colors do you remember, what smells come to mind? These are all questions to help you remember those highlights as well as aid you when sharing with others so they can experience the memory and celebrate with you. The more details you can remember and share with others, the more others can join into your story and be impacted by it.

Write It Down

When we remember our story, it is an opportunity to celebrate, but it also gives us strength to move forward. The further back we see, the farther in the future we can go. Remembering and sharing your story is as much about you as it is about others. Your story has the power to and will inspire others to overcome obstacles in their lives, give others courage to move through difficult moments, and remind them to celebrate the milestones in their life. That is why it's imperative that you know your story; you learn from it and inspire others when you share it. Sharing your story increases your self-awareness and actualization of what was and where you desire to go. Nelson Mandela emphasized moving forward with this notion when he said, "Remember to celebrate milestones as you prepare for the road ahead." Prepare for the road ahead and helping others prepare for the road ahead by sharing your story.

As you continue to navigate through the first step in the *SHIFT* framework, *Start Now*, you are building the foundation from which the other four steps will be created. Don't skim over this step; take the needed time to sit, remember, and process as you write out your story. Utilize this section of the book to write your story. Stop right now and begin to write your story by going through the six mile markers and using the questions in each section as a prompt to guide you.

All great teams and athletes have to start somewhere, and this is your starting point. You owe it to yourself to start well and lay a solid foundation that will give you a platform that will last for many years to come. Your Story is powerful and needs to be remembered and shared!

CHAPTER 3

ARE YOU A ONE-TRICK PONY?

Experience is the teacher of all things.

—Julius Caesar

Sitting in the coffee shop mid-morning, the athlete across from me has his hands covering his face as he shakes his head back and forth. The reality of a career-ending injury was starting to set in, and disbelief, frustration, anger, fear, and a sense of loss were racing through his mind and body. He has had an amazing career competing for over a decade as a professional athlete! Yet, here he was, lost, anxious, and fearful of what was to come. I will never forget the words he shared with me that morning.

"All I know is my sport, nothing else. I have nothing else to offer." There it was, the weight and reality that the dream and goal of playing professionally was all he knew, and now it was over at age twenty-nine. Can you relate? Have you felt that way before?

I once heard a pro athlete say something similar. "I am a one-trick pony. All I know is my sport." It makes sense when athletes feel like their sport is all they know and why athletes would believe that all they are good at is their sport. For the most part, as an elite athlete, you have invested thousands of hours and dollars toward your sport and competition, and you have been laser-focused on developing as an athlete. For most of your life, sport has been one of the most significant, time-consuming aspects of your life. But what you have learned and accomplished as an athlete doesn't have to fall by the wayside when you stop competing. All of that valuable experience can move with you beyond your sport and competition.

Tap Into Your Experience

It is amazing how the different aspects of our lives—mind, body, soul—intertwine to create us—and our lives. How well you perform can affect how you interact and navigate relationships or how you view yourself. The same is true coming from the other direction. If you have a struggling relationship, it can affect your decision making, how well you perform in competition, or even how you treat the support staff for your team.

I often hear about the importance of compartmentalizing, to create nice clean areas for each aspect of your life, so things don't get too complicated. Life is hard enough, and to have muddied areas makes things worse. Keeping each area of your life—relationships, education, your sport, family, etc.—separated into nice, neat different compartments is like trying to keep water in your hands when you put them under a water faucet.

You may be able to keep some water in your hands, but most of it finds a way to escape and go down the drain.

Athlete, you are not a one-trick pony. You have already looked at answering the questions about identity and rejecting the lie that you are what you do. You are so much more than your sport, your performance, what you own, or what people say about you. The power of your story is of significance, and that is why you must remember it, learn from it, and share it with others. As you rediscover your story and your history, more of it comes to life. The more you learn and study the *playbook*, the more familiar and connected you get with it. The more you remember and share your story, the more depth and richness it brings to your soul and to the lives of others.

That brings us to the third element of Start Now—your experience.

What Have You Experienced?

In his book *Outliers*, Malcolm Gladwell talks about the 10,000-hour rule; to become an expert at something, you must spend at least 10,000 hours practicing, training, and honing your skills as an athlete, musician, artist, etc. The 10,000-hour mark is a milestone that needs to be crossed, so you are able to move into the realm of expert. As an elite athlete, playing, training, and competing in your sport for sixteen-plus years, you have surpassed that milestone.

But all of those hours, even though focused on your sport, are not only about your sport. Your experience and character development as a result or bi-product of those thousands of hours are a valuable asset to you and those around you. Viktor Frankl, in his masterpiece

Man's Search for Meaning, shared about his experience in the concentration camps during World War II. He said, "Your experience is unique to you and that can't be taken away from you. I not only talk about the future and the veil drawn over it but also the past and its joys and how its light shines in the present darkness." He goes to quote a German poem. "What you have experienced, no power on earth can take from you." He finishes his thoughts on the value of one's past experiences by expounding that idea to say, "Not only experiences, but all of your thoughts, what you have done, great thoughts, all that you have suffered. Having being is also a kind of being and the surest kind of being."

Your experience, combined with your thoughts, actions, and choices, has culminated in bringing about success in your athletic life. The reality is those same experiences will also bring value, significance, and growth for whatever your next career is or when your next transition moment occurs. Don't dismiss your athletic experience or think you have to leave it all behind when you make the transition to life after sport. What you have accomplished, what you have invested—the time and energy—is not lost. It is the emotional and mental currency that has been growing and compounding interest for years. It is no wonder someone coined the phrase *wealth of experience*. In the appendix, there is a chart that shows some of the most valuable experience elite athletes have honed and collected over the years and how that experience will significantly impact and transfer over into your next career or arena.

Your experience has value, whether you were a life-long starter, came off the bench as a utility player, dealt with injuries throughout your career, were a captain, a role player, or any combination of those experiences and many more. Throughout your career, you had choices and experiences that have shaped you as a person and an athlete. The psychologist Carl Jung often shared about the quality of life related to the meaning one gives their experiences through choices, circumstances and the events experienced. He emphasized, "I am not what happened to me, I am what I choose to become." You are not only an athlete; you truly are more. Your experience and what you have navigated throughout your life by your choices, events, and circumstances have shaped you. What you bring to the table will only enhance and add exponentially to those in the room and on your future *team*. Your experience is unique to you—lessons learned, successes, failures, transitions, talents, character, abilities, personality, and choices. What will you choose today to become?

What you bring to the table will only enhance and add exponentially to those in the room and on your future *team*.

What Will You Do with Your Experience?

My wife Rachel loves to bake—cookies, crumbles, cakes, pies; you name it, she loves to bake it. Well, recently, she had a desire to learn how to bake artisan bread, which was going to add to the long list of amazing baked goods that often fill our home with enticing smells. Her love for baking is evident, but she wanted to stretch herself and try something new. So she bought some supplies, a few books, and materials to prepare. One of the items was a large two and one-half gallon bucket to store the dough. Part of the reason for the size is that you can prepare enough dough for multiple loaves. Well, the first time she made the bread, she mixed all of the ingredients together: flour, water, oil, eggs, salt, and yeast. After mixing everything together, she left all of the dough in the bucket on the counter to *rest*. During this *resting* time, the dough rose and nearly tripled in size. It was pretty cool to watch over the course of a few hours as the amount of dough continued to increase in size during its *rest*.

What's interesting is this same principle is true for humans. We are continuously collecting data, information, and *ingredients* each day. But what do you do with it all? I once heard a friend say he has forgotten more information than most people will ever learn in their lifetime. He was being a bit sarcastic, but the idea stuck with me. The amount of information we are inundated with each day is ridiculous, and the reality is that we forget most of it. We can thank our brains for that. Information gets categorized as it comes into our brains, and most information is then discarded and forgotten.

We already talked about the power of our stories—those moments of your story that are most memorable are filled with and have various emotions connected to that memory. Think about any great story that sticks in your memory, whether it be your own or someone else's or something you watch on TV. Regardless of it being a success story or a tragedy, there is an emotional experienced connected to it, which creates a sticking point in our minds. And that is what you want to create today, another chapter in your story that will be remembered for years to come. A turning point where you made a choice to maximize the transition to life beyond sport.

Start now. Don't wait.

There are moments in your life when you must force yourself to have your own *pre-season*, to slow down, go back over what's important, discover, and reinforce values, stories, and your identity. In *Start Now*, you are creating a moment to sit or *rest* on your identity, story, and experience—not only to solidify your life foundation but also to gain strength in your life. As an athlete, you have had the desire to play professionally or at the elite level for your entire life. You have thought, dreamed about, and *rested* with the idea that one day you will achieve that goal. You have daydreamed about hitting the walk-off home run, scoring the winning goal, or touching the wall before your opponent to win gold. As you spend time to *rest*, your identity, story, and experience will grow, increase and become clearer.

Now is the time to prepare for your next career, to transition well into life after sport, or simply transition to a new team and environment.

The first step in *SHIFT* is *Start Now*, and you are taking in all of what you bring to the table. In essence, you are mixing your ingredients and putting them into the bucket. Now that you have collected and mixed together all of the ingredients of your identity, your story, and your experience, they need to *rest*. While you put together the ingredients, allow them to sit in your mind. Thoughts, ideas, passions, new thoughts, and old thoughts will start to surface and come to light. As when you visualize your sport and what you desire to accomplish athletically, you will begin to see yourself moving, growing, and accomplishing within your next career.

You will remember a conversation you had when you were seventeen about a topic that was exciting to you but that you pushed aside to focus on your sport. Or perhaps you had an experience at university that brought joy to your soul and ignited a passion, but that was a *one-and-done* thing because it would have taken time away from training. As the dough rises as it rests, so will the ideas, thoughts, dreams, and experiences in you also rise. Through navigating this first step in *SHIFT*, you have compiled these elements to rise up, and it will become clearer how your experiences, thoughts, and ideas about what excites you brings life and gives you joy. In this first step, my hope is that you capture those thoughts. Get everything out on the table, write it all down, and don't hold back or dismiss your thoughts or ideas as you *Start Now*!

PART 2

HEART

Your vision will become clear only when you
look into your heart. Who looks outside,
dreams. Who looks inside awakens.

—Carl Jung

I am not a doctor, but I do know we all need our hearts.
Our hearts beat, and as they beat, blood is pumped
through our veins and arteries, throughout our bodies,
and into our brains. Without our hearts beating and
pumping, we would die. That may seem a bit obvious,
but there is value in understanding and recognizing the
simple basics of life.

This same reality is true for how you live out your
life. You have a physical heart, but you also have a *heart*
that is at the core of who you are and is what drives and
motivates you. I have lost count of the number of times
I have heard a teammate, athlete, coach, or parent say or
yell something along the lines of "that player competes

with heart," "she showed a ton of heart tonight," or "it takes heart to compete at this level." I imagine you have heard that as well!

Your athletic *heart* is the thing you possess and display in competition or training that creates moments where you can overcome or withstand something extremely difficult, whether it is finding victory, pushing through difficult environments to find athletic success, or finding the strength to increase your limits and blow through a 'PR.' Athletes want it and coaches look for it. It is an aspect of sport that is needed for success, but can you train and develop it? Do you know how to harness and leverage the drive and motivation that pushes you toward success and growth?

Your heart is at the core of your physical body; your *Heart* is also at the core of who you are and what drives and motivates you in life. There is an ancient proverb that encourages us to "Keep and guard your heart with all vigilance, for from it flow the springs of life."[4] Life springs forth from your heart, so let's go discover what makes your *Heart* beat!

CHAPTER 4

DISCOVER THE *COR* STRENGTH OF YOUR LIFE

To uncover your true potential you must first
find your own limits and then you have to have
the courage to blow past them.

—Picabo Street

I will never forget the first time I saw the beating hearts of my daughters through the ultrasound screen. It was amazing! You have a tiny screen with an image of a little body forming in the belly of her mother, and the nurse is slowly moving around the ultrasound magic wand and boom! There it is. A little beating heart, thumping like crazy. I never realized how much my heart would melt. I never knew how seeing the live action of my daughter's beating heart would affect my mind, heart, and soul in that moment. Our hearts and the hearts of others have power—emotionally and physically.

Your physical heart is continuously full. As blood full of nutrients is pumped out, blood that has flowed through arteries then returns to the heart through your veins, and the cycle continues. Everyone knows your heart is essential to life. Not only is your physical heart imperative for your survival and life as a human, but your metaphorical heart is also essential.

The heart of an athlete is the driving force for your purpose, meaning, desires, and calling. Your heart is at the core of who you are and why you do what you do. It is interesting that the Latin word for heart is *cor*. The center of the Earth is the core, and the center of an object, like an apple or a golf ball, is its core. It is the center of those objects, and it is essential for physical athletic success to have a strong core.

It is no wonder writers, philosophers, historians, athletes, educators, artists, musicians, and coaches alike have taken time to focus on the heart and to develop it, strengthen it, and grow it. Your heart is at the center of who you are and the energy source for what gets you up each day and drives you forward in good and difficult times. We all have it, but it also needs to be cultivated and grown. Like your physical heart is a muscle that can gain strength over time, so too, can your metaphorical heart grow.

Taking risks and pushing through the fear

I don't believe in coincidences! As I shared before, the Latin word for heart is *cor*. The root word for courage is also *cor*. The essence and center of courage is our heart! Courage comes from the heart, the center of our being. Winston Churchill stated, "Fear is a reaction. Courage is a decision." Courage doesn't come naturally to people; it is a cultivated and developed choice that builds momentum over time. You take a small step each day, and when faced with moments of fear or unknown, you choose to act courageously. Even sometimes, when you don't think you have what it takes, those small steps and actions built up over time surprise even yourself.

I don't know about you, but taking risks isn't something I set out to do every day. I don't wake up in the morning and tell myself, "I need to look for risks today and take them." More often than not, life happens, and risks and the opportunity to act with courage simply come up. When I was in high school, I ran the 300-yard hurdles in track. It was a difficult race mainly because of the timing. You had to have your steps down in between each hurdle. I remember innumerable times, counting in my head after each hurdle. *One, two, three, four, five, six, up,* over the hurdle and repeat. If my timing was off, things got dicey. If my kick was too early and I had too much space between myself and the hurdle, I would land on top of the hurdle. If my kick was too late, I would run through the hurdle rather than over. Either way, it would hurt, and it wasn't good!

I knew the distance between each hurdle, I knew the number of steps I needed to take, and I knew when to raise and kick my leg up and then propel the rest of my body over. Even then, my timing could be off, or a number of other things could go wrong, and I would struggle through the race. We can use sport to draw comparisons to life, and well, life is way harder!

Think of life this way. You are still running the 300-meter hurdles race but with one little difference. As you are running, random hurdles will pop out of the track at varying speeds, heights, and distances along the way. Sometimes you can see the hurdle ahead of you and have time to plan and adjust. Other times, a hurdle or hurdles will pop up right in front of you, and the next thing you know, you're face planting into the track. Life is unpredictable more often than not, and even though you try so hard to control your circumstances and the life around you, too many things that influence you are out of your control.

The civil rights activist and poet Maya Angelou had it right when she said, "The only thing is, people have to develop courage." Courage is needed, but it doesn't come naturally. It is developed intentionally over time. Your heart grows in strength when you increase your activity, training, fitness; your heart, your *cor*, also increases as you practice taking risks. Courage is the by-product of risk-taking, pushing through your fear, and as you practice taking risks, you are strengthening your heart and growing your courage from the inside out.

Find (or Define) Your Courage

Courage displayed reflects what is valued and important to you. When you are moved to action and display courage by taking risks, something inside of you is rising up. It could be doing the right thing at the right moment, standing up against injustice, fighting for something or someone who is unable to fight for themselves, providing water, clothing, or other needs for those who cannot provide for themselves. This list could go on endlessly. When you show courage, you are reflecting your heart and what you are passionate about in this life.

Famed author, speaker, and professor Brené Brown reinforces the importance of strengthening your heart and taking risks. "You can choose courage, or you can choose comfort, but you cannot choose both." As athletes, we know that to improve and grow in your sport and craft, you have to push yourself outside of your comfort zone. You have to be willing to take risks athletically to grow and find success in your sport. Those risks push your limits, your opportunities, and maximize your abilities.

Life will come at you! You will experience unforeseen circumstances, a death in the family, being cut from the team, a divorce—fill in the blank. Courage is developed over time, and you prepare for those courageous moments, not in the moment, but in the time leading up to those moments. Then you act, respond, and fight for what's right. Mark Twain reminds us that "Courage is resistance of fear, mastery of fear, not absence of fear." Those pivotal moments will come to pass, transitions will force your hand, *hurdles* will pop up, and you will show courage in those moments because your heart is strong! The first component to your heart is taking risks through courage. Your courage is reflected through your actions, but it begins on the inside, in your heart. Strengthen it and grow it by taking risks and acting courageously!

Harness the Power of Patience

Patience is your ability to be steadfast despite opposition, difficulty, or adversity. Even if you don't *feel* patience, I bet this is a trait you have developed. How do I know? Because you didn't get to where you are athletically in a day, a week, or even a year. You put in the work, navigate change, obstacles, setbacks, mountains that seem to come out of nowhere, or a steadily increasing incline slowly over time. Regardless of how you have experienced hardship over your life and athletic career, the power of patience is a necessary ingredient. Learning to unpack the reason or driving force behind your patience is key to clarifying your why, because it is in those moments of difficulty and struggle that you tap into something or someone to get you through.

Patience is not what I am known for. I want things now, and I want to see the results of my hard work and effort. I want what I want when I want it! As I am writing this, I am feeling a pull to check Instagram or see how the stock market is doing or how my most recent post on LinkedIn is growing in the number of *likes* and *shares*. I have to check myself, knowing that those quick little bursts of serotonin are giving me a false sense of accomplishment and are not truly achieving something of value.

Three Keys to Developing Patience

Patience is a quiet strength that increases over time. Famed martial arts expert Bruce Lee emphasized that when he said, "Patience is not passive. On the contrary, it is concentrated strength." Patience creates laser-like focus on what you are going after or what it is you are focusing on in your life. It allows you to eliminate the distractions on the outskirts of your vision so you can focus on what's most important. Here are three ways you can intentionally increase your patience.

1. Having a Clear Vision, Direction, and Reward

What is your future desire? It must be greater than your present reality. Whatever it is you are pursuing has to be larger and more grandiose than what you have accomplished, where you are, or what you are pursuing today. That is one of the main reason I tell athletes that their *why* has to be outside of themselves. If your why and driving force is about you, you have already capped off what you can accomplish and achieve. When your why is outside of yourself, you are forced to see the world, solve a problem, fight injustice, feed your family, or whatever it may be through a much larger lens than only yourself.

When you have a clear vision of what you hope to become it sets your direction forward through life. Once your direction is clear, your guide is set to aid in your navigation forward. This clarity brings into focus the reward you will receive once you reach your destination. Having a clear vision, direction, and reward gives you a reason to say *no* to the distractions of life that surround you—and they are everywhere.

2. Couple Inward Contentment with an Outward Discontentment

This may be a completely new perspective for you to consider. When you feel secure in your identity, you discover a new kind of strength. My challenge to you is to couple that strength with a discontentment you feel with your character, actions, mindset, or outcomes. Contentment of self and who you are doesn't change, but knowing what it looks like to be at your best is still beyond your fingertips. You can see it, envision it, taste it, but it is not quite a reality yet. You possess patience when you know who you are; now, you are on the road to becoming what and who you desire to be and heading where you want to go.

Carol Dweck, well-known professor at Stanford University and author of *Mindset*, talks about the growth mindset, which is the idea that what we experience in life can be used as an opportunity to grow, progress, and develop. The growth mindset sees life's obstacles, difficulties, and setbacks as moments in time to get better and improve. Having this growth mindset is interrelated to one's patience and ability to see the greater value of growth moving forward rather than stopping because sport, life, and relationships are hard or difficult. Dweck states, "In this mindset, the hand you're dealt is just the starting point for development. This growth mindset is based on the belief that your basic qualities are things you can cultivate through your efforts. Although people may differ in every which way—in their initial talents and aptitudes, interests, or temperaments—everyone can change and grow through application and experience." It merely takes time and patience to stay the course and see your best true self come to fruition!

Having an inward contentment gives strength and acknowledgment of who you are while still giving you the confidence that you can continue to grow, develop, and progress over time. One of the commonalities of those with a growth mindset is they love what they do. Dweck reiterates that by saying, "The growth-mindset athletes, CEO's, musicians, or scientists all loved what they did. They got to the top as a result of doing what they loved. It's ironic: The top is where the fixed-mindset people hunger to be, but it's where many growth-minded people arrive as a by-product of their enthusiasm for what they do." There was passion and drive that came from the depths of their souls and their hearts! It fueled the desire to keep going, to be patient, and to see failures as learning opportunities, knowing that the present reality was not their future destiny.

Whether you have already retired and moved on from your sport, are early in your career, or somewhere in between, be patient. The transitions in life and sport can be planned for or sometimes come out of nowhere.

Either way, an inward contentment with an outward discontentment will give you the patience and fortitude to keep moving forward.

3. Work with a Life Coach

As athletes, the coach is someone who has been a part of your life almost as far back as you can remember. I remember being four years old when I first experienced sport and coaching. Even though it was my dad at that moment, I still remember him carrying the dual titles of coach and dad. The role of a coach has many facets. Great coaches dig deep into the souls of athletes and bring out greatness that the athlete doesn't yet recognize or see in themselves. They inspire, motivate, cultivate, and bring out the best in you as an athlete and person. Well, coaching isn't only reserved for sport; coaching can be a part of every aspect of your life, whether it is focusing on your leadership, character, life, faith, or sport.

When you begin to think about and clarify your why, a coach is a valuable asset to helping you discover your why and what drives you. Seeking out a life coach, a character coach, or a transition coach will help you navigate the process of clarifying your why. Your athletic coach was able to bring out the best in you within competition, and a coach can help bring clarity to your passion, purpose, and why. When your athletic coach shows you a trophy or tells a story about where she has taken players in the past, there is a confidence that develops as you hear the story. The same is true for coaches outside of your sport. There is power when you identify someone who has already walked down the path you desire to go and has experienced navigating through this new unknown territory you want to explore.

I heard it once said that a coach can influence more people in a year than the average person does in a lifetime. The influence can be either positive or negative. Coaches impact athletes' lives each and every day. So, when thinking about life after sport and transition, doesn't it make sense to seek out a coach to help you in the process? Coaches have helped you navigate through the ups and downs of your sport and maybe have impacted you beyond your sport. When I was playing at Ohio Wesleyan University, Dr. Jay Martin, the head coach, would often talk about us being people, then students, and athletes. What he knew and imprinted on me was that, eventually, my athletic career would end, but my humanity would last a lifetime. He wanted to develop and grow great people with strong values and character who also simply happened to be successful in sport!

Jay is now the winningest coach in NCAA men's soccer history. Winning isn't his main focus. People are. Jay would continue to emphasize our character and leadership, knowing it would fuel and build stronger athletes. The results and success of wins and losses was a natural effect of the character and leadership he focused on within the program. Jay had coached long enough to know that our athletic careers would eventually come to an end, but being human and impacting our world would last our lifetime. So, he focused on developing good, strong, healthy people, and again, winning became a by-product of that development.

I realize not all athletic coaches have the same perspective as Jay. That is why it is important for you to find a coach or mentor to help navigate through the transitions in sport, to help you build a practice of patience in your life, and to help you prepare you for life after sport and the opportunities in front of you.

Clarifying Your *Why*

The core of who you are is your heart, and what keeps your heart pumping is your *why*. Your *why* brings about passion, desire, willingness, and action. Your *why* is on display in the critical moments of your life. You can reflect on what you accomplished and celebrate and sometimes even ask yourself, "Did I do that? Did I accomplish or overcome that?" You look back and hit pause and ask, "Was that really me?" Your *why* is your fuel that drives you forward in times of uncertainty. When you know your *why*, your way comes to life. It is like the illuminated path that lights up on the aisle of the airplane when the lights go out to show you where to walk.

So how do you clarify, discover, and recognize your *why*?

You have begun this journey of discovery and self-awareness, and the

> "Be yourself. Everyone else is taken." — Oscar Wilde

essence of this journey is growing in your understanding of self and what it means to be you. The easiest way to discover your *why* is by asking yourself two questions. Your *why* is something inside of you because you are special and unique. Your *why* is personal, uniquely you, so don't compare yourself to those around you; that will quickly erode who you are and the power you possess. Oscar Wilde said it well. "Be yourself. Everyone else is taken."

To define your why, consider two essential questions:
Who am I?
Whose am I?

Each one of us is uniquely created and uniquely built. You have certain gifts and talents and abilities. You have certain passions, desires, perspectives—even your fingerprints are unique. There are billions of people around the world, and there is only one you! How cool is that? And so, your heart, your *why*, comes from that uniqueness. That's really the focus of wanting to explore what you are passionate about. What do you desire? What comes from your core? What drives you? That is your *why*!

It is imperative you answer the two questions because life often tries to answer those questions for you; for example, life may tell you that to be valued, you must do certain things, wear specific clothes, or act in different ways than you would ordinarily. How you speak, where you grew up, the color of your skin, Adidas or Nike—how society and sport culture define you can be an endless list. You are more than the sport you play. It's time to stand up! But it is difficult to stand if you don't know who you are. So, *who are you?*

Whose am I? is making the statement of who or what you worship. And yes, the thought of worship may bring about some religious connotations or some tribal ritual, but we all worship something or someone, whether or not you call it worship. I define worship as an extravagant respect or admiration for or a devotion to a person, place, or thing. So, what are you worshipping? *Whose are you?*

To what in your life have you given extravagant respect or admiration? What are you fully devoted to in your life? For me, it was my sport! I was willing to push people, events, opportunities, and relationships aside for my sport. I worshipped soccer, and the stadiums and playing grounds became my place of worship.

Here is the power of your *why*. When there is a perspective shift for you from *this sport is what I do, who I am, and what I worship*, to *this sport is what gives me an opportunity to impact life and those I love*. A shift to realize sport gives you the opportunity to reflect what you are created to do—your abilities and character—and that sport is an opportunity to speak and shed light on an issue you want to tackle and solve, to become a solution to problems in your world. Your sport and performance turn from being what you worship to the catalyst of impact and change you desire for your world—and your *why* is at the epicenter of impact and change. Remember, your why needs to be outside of yourself; otherwise you cap and limit what you can truly accomplish.

Because you are you, and I am me, I can't tell you what your why is or what it should be. Your *why* is unique to you. It is your driving force and comes from your heart. To help you clarify your why, I have put together ten questions to aid you in the process. A little reminder before you answer them is when your *why* goes beyond yourself, the power of it grows and is stronger than when it is focused solely on yourself.

Ten Questions to Identify Your Why

1. What are the things you enjoy doing?
2. What drains you rather than fuels you?
3. Where do you feel most at home? What type of environment or place provides you with inspiration or energy?
4. What has been shared with you that resonates as true?

5. What attitudes or behaviors are so natural to you that you do them without thinking, and time passes by?

6. What dreams have you dreamt that you can't forget? They may not be at the forefront of your mind, but they come to mind consistently over the years.

7. What are your natural talents, or what comes easily for you?

8. Take an assessment (strengths finder, enneagram, Meyers-Briggs, etc.). What does it say about you?

9. Who do you feel most connected to? What types of people do you feel drawn to serve or support?

10. For what problem, issue, or cause do you want to be part of the solution?

Knowing Your Why Makes You Unbreakable

The movie *Unbroken* is set during World War II in the Pacific Theater. Louis "Louie" Zamperini, who competed in the 1936 Olympics for the USA in track and field, was flying in a B-52 bomber on a rescue mission when his bomber crash-landed in the Pacific Ocean. After surviving forty-seven days on a raft, the Japanese captured Louie and sent him to a number of prisoner of war (POW) camps.

While in Omri, a POW camp near Tokyo, the Japanese corporal Mutshiro "The Bird" Watanabe oversaw the camp. The Bird incessantly berated Louie and often would beat him. At one point, he discovered that Louie had competed in the Olympics and forced him to race another officer around the camp. Louie was beaten, significantly dehydrated, and malnourished, but willed himself to race and compete. Watanabe eventually was promoted to another post, and Louie believed the worst was behind him.

As the Americans continued to fight the Japanese in the Pacific theater, the US was pushing the Japanese troops closer to their homeland. Zamperini was eventually shipped to another POW camp, Naoestsu, when Tokyo was bombed. That was where Watanabe was promoted to Sergeant and now in command. At Naoestsu, the prisoners were required to work as slave labor, loading coal onto barges.

In one scene, Louie pauses from the brutal work. Watanabe sees him and punishes him. Watanabe forces Zamperini to lift a large log above his head and tells another solder if he drops it to shoot him. Louie lifts the log above his head and, in utter defiance, stares at Watanabe while holding the log. Zamperini finds strength from somewhere and continues to hold the heavy log over his head. Enraged, Watanabe finally beats Zamperini, and the powerful moment is over.

Zamperini often thought about his family, and he possessed an incredible desire to return home. That fueled his will to live and survive the unbearable circumstances, beatings, and lack of food and water. Zamperini had a *why* that fueled his survival, and in that moment of defiance, holding up that log, mustered up the tenacity that not only gave him strength but also the other prisoners at the camp. Zamperini's story is an amazing testament of what someone can endure, accomplish, the character he possessed, and what can be displayed when you know your *why*.

So what's inside of you? I am guessing that neither you nor I will ever experience a POW camp, but there will be setbacks, struggles, injury, pain, and hurt. When life goes sideways, having a clear *why* gives you strength, grit, and fortitude to keep going, push through, and overcome the circumstance you are experiencing.

Start with Why author, Simon Sinek, reinforces this reality when he says, "Knowing your WHY is not the only way to be successful, but it is the only way to maintain a lasting success and have a greater blend of innovation and flexibility. When a WHY goes fuzzy, it becomes much more difficult to maintain the growth, loyalty and inspiration that helped drive the original success." Your heart is at the center of who you are and your *why*.

There is a chant from fans at soccer games that says, "Who are you, who are you, who are you?" Usually, this is yelled after a player makes a mistake, bad pass, missed shot, or a give-away, etc. The fans are questioning who you are and your abilities. The statement is simple and clear, mocking and making fun of the player. You messed up—who are you, why are you on the field? They are bringing up the question and doubt of who you are and your impact.

In sport and life, we all experience difficult circumstances that are completely out of our control, but at the core of each experience, the same key component is necessary—a strong Heart. Your heart is developed and strengthened when you have and grow your courage, cultivate patience in your life, and have a clear *why*. That is the reason it is of the utmost importance to protect your heart with all vigilance, for from it flows the springs of life. Your heart is the driving force that gives you the strength to press on and overcome those difficult moments in sport and in life. Know your *why*!

CHAPTER 5

UNDERSTANDING THE LENS THROUGH WHICH YOU VIEW YOUR LIFE

You're only as good as your values.

—Herb Brooks

A picture can say a thousand words, as the old saying goes. Whether you love utilizing your filters on Instagram, Photoshop, or on your favorite photo editing app, it is amazing what you can do to an image to make it stand out! Years ago, while I was in university, I picked up photography. The camera was an old Nikon, and I envisioned myself taking amazing photos and having them framed and up on the wall for all to see in some famous gallery. I was a little overconfident in my abilities and what I was actually producing. Something that was interesting to me was the use of filters (not like the filters on apps). When using a camera, on the end of the lens you can attach a filter that affects how the picture turns out. There were magnifying filters, colored filters with red, blue, orange, yellow, polarized filters, and many other options. My favorite was the yellow filter. I'm not sure exactly why, but I liked how the yellow filter affected the photo and how it changed the picture visually.

I know that photography and taking pictures has changed significantly over the past twenty years; I was using real film when I started and remembered taking a roll of film to the store to be developed; I could even pay a little extra to have the roll developed in an hour. Nowadays, you have instant access to the picture you take through your phone or digital camera and a myriad of editing options. As much as I enjoyed putting on those lenses, waiting hours or days, and finally seeing the effects of the filter on the picture, I do prefer how today's technology works and being able to see the effects of the filters change instantly!

I am guessing you have used a filter on your phone for Instagram, Snapchat, Facebook, or to edit your photos. Chances are you are answering with a sarcastic, "Yes." I don't even remember the last time I didn't scroll through the filters to see what the picture I took looks like with *Juno*, *Clarendon*, *Ludwig*, or *Lark*. Or when I didn't look to see how the picture would appear if I added funky sunglasses or cute little stars floating around my face with accompanying sparkles.

Filters have become a staple in our lives, images, and on social media, but have you thought about what filters are in your life or as an athlete? Is there a *Juno* filter effect that helps create a more vibrant color palette for how you experience life and the hours of your day? Or is there a filter when you train or how you compete in games? When you add a filter to the picture, it changes and adjusts the image, and your life is much the same.

Your personal values are like filters for your life and your experiences. Your values affect and change how you see, experience, and remember events and moments in time. That is the reason two people who experience the same event, game, or circumstance can have two different memories or views of that event. Whether it is sport, politics, economics, race, or any other number of circumstances, your values shape what you observe, experience, value, and remember.

What are values?

Values impact and influence your behavior, thought processes and decisions, your attitude, and how you interact and engage with other people. Your values affect, influence, and impact visually every aspect of your life. So, do you know what your values are? Maybe you do, but from my experience, most athletes, and people for that matter, don't know their personal values. Ironically, if your values truly affect decisions, attitudes, and relationships, shouldn't we all know what our values are so we can recognize how they are impacting situations, circumstances, and life in general?

The obvious answer is *yes*, but again, few athletes know what their values are. My experience has been athletes and teams have identified a handful of cool or popular values based on who has influenced them. Or some use what some famous coach or athlete has stated are their value, like excellence, respect, courage, teamwork, or loyalty. What happens when you graduate, leave that team, or are traded? I guess you could adapt to the values of the new team or club, but with each change, that only adds confusion as you transfer from one team to the next or onto your career after competing.

When you take on values from outside of yourself, there isn't much depth to them. The values become a mile wide but an inch deep, losing any significance or meaning for you personally. Talking about the values of your current team may sound good to the media or online, but the values are not of value to you, so there is no internalization or ownership of the values. And that is not who you are; you have depth, significance, and ownership of self. Therefore, knowing your personal values will create natural outcomes in your life that will align with your values and go beyond your sport and competition. Clarifying your values will impact you today and for the rest of your life. In addition, your values will establish a ripple effect that will impact your actions, attitudes, choices, and mentality, but also the lives of your teammates, friends, family, fans, coaching staff, and community.

Eight Outcomes of Knowing Your Values

Clarity—When you have clarity of mind and movement, you are able to overcome obstacles and difficulties that you encounter in life and sport. When you don't know your values, your vision and ability to see clearly diminishes, resulting in poor decisions and seeking significance and connection from people, substances, or objects that will never give you what you need or want. Philosopher Blaise Pascal shared, "Clarity of mind means clarity of passion, too; this is why a great and clear mind loves ardently and sees distinctly what it loves." Values are like the morning sun as it burns the morning fog away, allowing you to see clearly the beauty and steps before you.

Courage—Courage can take on different forms and actions. The willingness to sit and listen and show empathy is truly a courageous act. It demonstrates to the other person that you care and value them for who they are and where they are at in life. As athletes, courage is thought of more in regard to actions on the court or field or those moments when no one is watching. Courage is also knowing when to see your world through the lens of another. Winston Churchill highlighted that when he said, "Courage is what it takes to stand up and speak; courage is also what it takes to sit down and listen." Knowing your values is knowing who you are. When you know who you are, you will have greater freedom to sit and listen and focus on someone else.

Security—When you understand what you are all about and what you bring to the table for your team, there is a security and confidence that comes to the forefront. A sense of belonging to something bigger than yourself, one piece of a completed puzzle. The same is true with knowing and clarifying your values. In times of chaos, knowing your values gives you a security to be yourself and not put on a mask to hide or attempt to morph into someone or something else. Knowing your values as an athlete gives you a foundation to build on as you compete, as well as how you interact with your coach and teammates in the locker room and off the court. Author Stephen Covey, in *The 7 Habits of Highly Successful People*, wrote, "Security represents your sense of worth, your identity, your emotional anchorage, your self-esteem, your basic personal strength or lack of it." Competing and living in freedom is a result of being secure in who you are and acting like yourself while engaging with others. Knowing your values allows you to compete and live from a place of security.

Consistency—In sport, consistency is liquid gold. I have heard numerous times from coaches that they would rather have an athlete that performs at a *six* every day than an athlete who is an *eight* one day and then a *three* the next. With the latter, the coach doesn't know which athlete will show up for the game, but with the athlete who is consistent, the coach knows what to expect and the results they will get from her. The better you know yourself and the more attuned you are to your values, the more consistent you become as a person and as an athlete. I agree with Dwayne "The Rock" Johnson when he says, "Success isn't always about greatness. It's about consistency. Consistent hard work gains success. Greatness will come." Consistency is essential to success, and knowing your values will allow you to be at your best regardless of the circumstance you find yourself.

> "Success isn't always about greatness. It's about consistency. Consistent hard work gains success. Greatness will come."
> — Dwayne Johnson

Excitement—I love to compete, and I am guessing you do as well. The opportunity to play and compete gets my blood pumping and excites me. But what I have learned is that knowing my values has intensified my excitement to play the game. Let me explain a bit more. Knowing your values allows you the freedom to leverage and use your emotions and channel them into your competition, training, or even the media conference after a game. Clarifying your values helps shift your perspective from a *have to* to a *get to* mentality. You will still experience the emotions, but they are shifted to excitement rather than fear. To be honest, there is a similar effect in life as a whole going through an interviewing process, starting a new job, or working to start a company or non-profit.

Knowing your values does not diminish the pressures of life or anxiety, but your values will get you excited about those pressure moments and see them as opportunities to grow and develop. Robert Kiyosaki, author of *Rich Dad, Poor Dad* and business owner, emphasized the importance of this reality by saying, "Don't let the fear of losing be greater than the excitement of winning." Knowing your values will grow your excitement.

Guidance—Have you ever heard the saying, "Let your values be your guide?" The meaning of that statement comes about and is shared when people experience difficult or unknown moments in their life. In those moments of struggle, uncertainty, and chaos, allow your values to direct and guide your steps. That sounds great, but what if you don't know your values or you only have some arbitrary idea of what they are? Then the saying is not helpful. When things go sideways or hit the fan or however you want to describe these types of life situations, your values help guide your steps. If you are not intentional in those moments of chaos, you may end up somewhere or in a situation you don't want. Lao Tzu stated, "If you don't change direction, you may end up where you are headed." When stress is all around you, you react and make quick or rash decisions: fight, freeze, or flight. Your values create an anchor for you and give you a foundation to build and move forward in the midst of uncertainty. They guide you!

Significance—When you focus on the results, you buy into the lie that who you are and your value is based on your performance. The destination of performance and results becomes the focus, rather than the process and the journey. Knowing your values helps you recognize that the journey is the destination, and those small steps you take each day are important and have value. Oprah Winfrey emphasized this point when she said, "The key to realizing a dream is to focus not on success but significance—and then even the small steps and little victories along your path will take on greater meaning." It is easier to measure the results and the clear data. Significance is not only measured through the lens of data; one small action can be significant to one person yet not another. The reason is people see life through the filter of their values. When you know your values, the small steps of significance become clearer and more recognizable to you.

Connection—Values create bridges to cover gaps between your relationships and connections with others. Knowing your values will give you the confidence to be yourself while you interact and engage with others. Knowing your values gives you the freedom to navigate tension, conflict, and shared experiences where you can give of yourself and not feel like you need to wear a mask and cover your true self. Author and professor Brené Brown shares, "I define connection as the energy that exists between when they feel seen, heard, and valued; when they can give and receive without judgment; and when they derive sustenance and strength from the relationship." When you know yourself, it is easier for you to connect with those around you because you are coming from a place of confidence. As an athlete, confidence is essential for how you walk out onto the field, court, track, or wherever your competitive space is, as well as in life. Confidence is a result of connection and a sense of belonging!

Knowing your values clarifies how and where you navigate through the interpersonal relationships around you. Being a good teammate is important for team chemistry so you are able to perform collectively at your best. In addition, knowing your values gives clarity as you work with others after your career is over.

Refine Your Filter

Let me share a brief story to illustrate the importance of team dynamics and knowing your values. When I was seventeen, I was invited to play on a new team where a majority of the players had been together for a few years. Because the core of players had been around for a while, it didn't take long for the new players to mesh quickly with the rest of the team. There was one player who was extremely frustrating to me. But I wasn't sure why. Off the field, we got along great. He was a chill guy, very personable, and he accepted me and was intentional to bring me into the team dynamic. For whatever reason, on the field, I found myself frustrated with him as a player.

Recently, I was doing some soul searching and reflecting on my values and how they influenced me as an athlete. I was taking time to meditate on my values and remember how my actions and mentality were impacted by my values, specifically early in my career. I was thinking about this time of transition at age seventeen and being invited to this new team, and those frustrating moments came to mind. I was only on that team for one season, but the memories of my frustration were vivid.

As an athlete, I wasn't always the most talented, but I always put in the work, no matter what. Hard work and a strong work ethic were important to me, and I took that same mentality into training and competition. What I learned about myself as I was meditating and reflecting on those early years is that work ethic is one of my values. You get up early, put in the work, and give it everything you've got. Even in my writing, that is true. While I am writing this book, I have been getting up early before the kids wake up. It's dark outside and quiet in the house so that I can focus on my writing. You have to put in the work and get things done!

Back to the story. This teammate didn't work hard in trainings. During the game, he was fantastic, great work rate, very talented and technical. In training, he acted as if he didn't care. He would sort of warm up with the rest of the team, he would mess around during training, acting like he didn't really want to be there, and it drove me crazy. It didn't make sense to me why he would act this way. I was experiencing and seeing this teammate and his actions through the filter of my value of having a strong work ethic.

At the time, I didn't fully know what was making me so frustrated and angry with this teammate. Reflecting back at this time and many others like it have helped me understand the power and impact of my values on my life, and the same is true for you. Remember, your values are the filter through which you view and experience life. Like the various filters on Instagram change the effects of the image, your values change how you view, observe, and experience life.

Be Secure Enough to Be Self-Aware

Clarifying and knowing your personal values starts with self-awareness. Being self-aware gives you an open window into who you are, what makes you unique and how you function. If you look back at the first few chapters about identifying your core beliefs, understanding your identity, and writing out your story and your experience, there is an overlap that occurs.

I am writing this book in 2020 during the COVID 19 pandemic. As I have journeyed with a number of professional athletes during this time, it has been intriguing how each athlete responds to the pandemic, not playing or training as a team, and the reality of playing games in empty stadiums without fans. The importance of knowing yourself and being self-aware of what makes you is powerful. I tell my kids that we all have power, and the better we know ourselves, the less of our own power we give away frivolously to others.

Let me explain what I mean when I say giving your power away to someone else. When we get angry and lash out at someone, we are giving our power away to that individual. We are allowing their actions to dictate our actions through our response. You are responsible for your emotions, actions, responses, and words. You are giving your power away to someone else when you allow another individual's actions to control you. You have now given them authority over you by responding or acting like someone who is not your best self. You are giving your power away when you say something like, "She made me do that," or "You make me feel angry or sad." You always have a choice; don't allow others to take control over your power. It is yours to give freely and live your best.

Knowing your values gives you confidence to be you and not put up a front and be someone or something you are not. As athletes, knowing yourself gives you the confidence to compete at a high level, even if things are not going well. I have heard multiple times from basketball players how their coaches responded to poor shooting when the players were having an off night. When asked after the game, they told the reporter that their coach said simply to keep shooting! I was given the same advice when I was playing. I was having an off night, and I couldn't make a basket if my life depended on it, but my coach told me to keep shooting until the shots started going in.

Being self-aware gives you the freedom not to focus on the immediate results, but to focus on who you are and the process. That's why coaches tell shooters to keep shooting the ball, especially on *off* nights—because that's what players and shooters do. They shoot and score. Being self-aware and knowing your values gives you the confidence to keep going, even in those difficult moments in sport and in life, and your values give you the confidence to be yourself and at your best consistently.

Be True to Yourself

As a direct result of your values, your influence and impact in the world go beyond the game you play. When writing about the historic and successful team, the All Blacks, New Zealand's famed rugby team, James Kerr, in his book *Legacy*, sheds light on this reality. "Character rises out of your values, our purpose, the standards we set for ourselves, our sacrifice and commitment, and the decisions we make under pressure, but it is primarily defined by the contribution we make, the responsibility we take, and the leadership we show." Your values affect the standards you set for your sport and yourself, where you put the bar, and what your level of commitment is to achieve and compete at that level. Your values also affect how you make decisions, the speed and confidence of your decision making, your willingness to take risks, to make mistakes, and to own and learn from them.

The impact you make as a human goes beyond the game. Whether or not you want the role; youth, adults, and society are looking up to you and watching your behavior and your words. You are a role model, and your values will shed light on how you handle and navigate the responsibility for your actions on and off the field, as well as the ripple effect and impact on the lives of those around you.

I have added a worksheet in the appendix to help clarify and identify your personal values. It is a simple process but not an easy one. It is worth the effort, though, to know your values because they are the filter through which you compete and live out your life.

So, what do you value? Knowing what your top values are will provide you with a better understanding of who you are and what makes you function as a human. Your values are the filter through which you see the world around you. Understanding those filters gives clarity to how you view, think, respond, and act and make a difference in your world.

CHAPTER 6
LIFE THEMES: EXPLORING YOUR *DÉJÀ VU* EXPERIENCES

Outstanding people have one thing in common:
An absolute sense of mission.

—Zig Ziglar

There is poetry in motion in sport when transitions occur. Whether it is the beauty of *turning two* in the double play in baseball, the counterattack in soccer that ends with a goal, or a rebound and quick outlet pass and the alley-top dunk, it's beautiful to see. When a transition happens, there are quick decisions that need to be made, preparation that is essential to maximize those moments before they are lost, confidence needed to take that decisive action, and finally, the strength and fortitude to execute and see results. Athletically, you take the time to prepare and focus on those moments. Hours are spent training and planning for that brief moment on the track and the relay race on when and how to make a clean handoff. Weeks and multiple training sessions are focused on what to do when you lose the ball in basketball or soccer or how you will respond when you make a mistake; will you bounce back, take advantage of the mistake of your opponent and find success?

All of these moments of transition in sport are small yet significant! When we examine our lives, the same is true. There are moments of decision, action-filled with fear, unknowns, and chaos where action is needed. But what makes athletes and teams successful in those times of transition is the time spent before that moment occurs. The work has been put in creating clarity and identity of self and the team, which allows for action to take place.

This book is focused on assisting you in maximizing those moments of transition—whether they are decisions about food, meal prep, buying a car, how you respond when you make a mistake or hurt a friend, the transitions of job change, moving to a new city or country, off-seasons, a trade, buying a house, or nearly anything else.

What gives you the freedom to take risks and maximize those moments of transition are knowing your heart and what fuels your passion as well as what excites you and gives you life. In the previous two chapters, we have looked at clarifying your why and identifying your core values. Our hope is to protect your heart with all vigilance, for from it comes the springs of life. There is passion and desire in your heart, and we want to zero in and let it out. Your heart is the engine that brings your soul to life and the drive to action and character.

Remember that your heart is vital to your athletic success, and your heart is vital to a quality, successful, and well-lived life. I don't know about you, but my desire when I woke up this morning was to make a difference, to impact people positively, to see lives changed for the good, and to impact the world around me. How I do that will look different than how you do it, but can you imagine what our teams, clubs, and communities would look like if everyone woke up inspired, looking forward to impacting their world positively, to bring light and joy rather than darkness and despair or settle for mediocrity? It would transform our world.

The third aspect of your heart is *Life Themes.* Themes in our life are like train tracks; they help guide and direct the train to go toward a destination. The tracks need to be laid down in order for the train to run on them, and that is what you are doing now; you are laying the tracks on which your life train will run. You are not one-sided, one size fits all. Everyone has differing passions and desires and hopes. An athletes' focus is more or less on the sport or the actions and decisions made directly related to that sport and competition, like weight training, film and video analysis, nutrition, and recovery. Those are secondary actions with the primary focus on the sport and athletic performance. Competition and playing the sport you love and appreciate has been one goal you have strived to achieve, and for many, since a very young age.

Been there. Seen that. Living it again.

Have you ever taken the time to think about something other than your sport or training? What other passions and desires do you have that are not related to your sport? Perhaps an activity or experience that was difficult yet fulfilling? Or maybe there was another action that came more easily to you because of your talent and abilities? What if there was something else beyond your sport? What if you discovered that there is something outside of the game that brings you joy, stirs up a passion, and motivates you? Your heart is dynamic, and it is the driving force of your life, and the thought that you are only an athlete is crazy. You are truly more than an athlete!

I define *Life Themes* as an idea, thought, or subject that recurs in one's story or permeates within and throughout a person's life. It's an indication or the main subject of a person's thoughts and life experience. Whether or not you have realized that, everyone's life has themes running through it. These ideas, thought, and actions that continually come up in your life, behaviors, and environments. It is like experiencing a *déjà vu* moment. The phrase is French and translates as "already seen." The phrase and the meaning behind it are essentially that you have lived through this moment before. It's that eerie sensation you get when you feel you have been to a restaurant or met a person or lived the current situation you are presently experiencing before in your life. So that we are all on the same starting point, a theme is an idea or subject that recurs in or permeates throughout a person's behavior, thoughts, works of art, or sport.

It's time to go discover and see what themes have been running through your life. I bet there will be some surprise at what is already inside of you and what surfaces. As you go through this process, it will grow and strengthen you as an athlete, but importantly as a human.

Three Actions to Clarify and Identify Your Life Themes

1. Recognize the consistencies throughout your story.

Earlier in the book, we looked at your identity and the power of your story. Let's take a closer look there first to begin to identify your life themes. Your story will begin to illuminate those reoccurring ideas and thoughts in your life. So, stop right now, and go get your story that you wrote down from chapter two. Get it out and read over it. What jumps out at you? Are there ideas or thoughts that reoccur when you write through the Six H's? Your story is a window into your soul, your driving force, what you are passionate about, and what you focus in on and remember. Harold Whitman talked about this when he said, "Don't ask yourself what the world needs; ask yourself what makes you come alive. Then go do that because the world needs people who have come alive." What are the things, experiences, and moments that have made you come alive in sport and in life?

Taking that closer look at your story, what are those moments that continue to pop up and are intertwined throughout your story? My guess is that as you revisit your story, more memories will come to mind that align with what you have written down. Capture those moments too, and add them to your story. Remember what Winston Churchill said. "The farther backward you can look, the farther forward you can see." When you know your life themes, it gives you clarity and decisive action as you move forward. Like in sport, you are able to respond instantly to change and maximize those moments. My hope is that you are able to do the same in your life—maximize and make the most of all that life throws at you!

When I remember my story, there are a few moments early on that stick out to me. One of my life themes is coach/teacher. When I was in high school, I began to realize I enjoyed teaching and helping others grow and learn. Whether it was on the athletic field or basketball court or in the classroom, seeing and experiencing someone learn something new brought joy to my soul. I even started my own youth soccer camp in the winter of my junior year of high school to work with other youth in the community. I had an internal desire to help other athletes grow, develop, improve, and grow their understanding of the sport. Looking back, I see an irony in that soccer was a sport played for recreation, but not many played beyond the age of twelve or thirteen. There was no local soccer club to compete with, and my development wasn't that far beyond many of the other kids, but my desire was to help and coach others to improve and introduce them to the sport and game I loved.

By reflecting on your story, it illuminates moments in time to reveal themes that will reoccur in your life. Your life is not fully linear or separate from one aspect to the other. Your story, values, heart, and life themes, while unique, also overlap with each other, which makes up the beauty of who you are and who are you created to be on this Earth. So, take advantage of that reality as you are looking to identify your life themes and look for patterns in your story, moments, and experiences when you were at your best.

2.   Identify what inspires and stirs your soul.

What are the memories when you felt inspired and your soul was stirred with emotion? When were those moments where you came alive and passion overflowed through your actions and created more intentional actions? When you come alive, you are strengthening and highlighting your why and fueling your drive and passions. In essence, you are developing and strengthening your *Heart* muscle. Physical fitness grows your heart and endurance; the same principle applies with your *Heart*; the more action you take within your passion, the stronger it becomes.

> "Passion is the thing that will help you create the highest expression of your talent."
> — Dr. Larry Smith

Passion is an indication you are experiencing and living out one of your life themes. Carmine Gallo is a popular keynote speaker, author of seven books, and a communication coach who wrote an article about why TED Talks are wildly addictive. She spent hundreds of hours studying, researching, looking at brain scans and hours of TED Talk presentations to discover the reason behind TED talks and their success. In her article, she discusses the first scientific reason, namely that 'passion is contagious.' Gallo highlights University of Waterloo economics professor Dr. Larry Smith in his TED Talk entitled "Why You Will Fail to Have a Great Career." Dr. Smith shared that "Passion is the thing that will help you create the highest expression of your talent." What's amazing is that as I wrote this, Dr. Smith's talk has been viewed nearly seven million times. Gallo doesn't mince words; she states, "Smith's message is simple: Follow your passion and you will have a great career. Don't follow it and you won't."

You might be thinking, *Jonathan, I am passionate about my sport and really nothing else.* I can understand where you are coming from when making that statement, but I would guess there is something about the sport and competition that makes you come alive. Maybe it is the process of development and improvement, the relational connection, the opportunity to build a team and find success, achieving goals and reaching milestones throughout the season, seeing hard work pay off, working together as a team, or the struggle and difficulty of bringing people together from various countries, cultures, languages and getting them all to buy into a common goal and vision. The list of reasons for being passionate about your sport is significant. When you explore and identify your life themes, you are looking at the specifics of what you are passionate about, so look for those specifics of why you are passionate about your sport and competition. What is it that brings your soul to life as you compete?

Watch the Whole Film

You wouldn't watch game film of a victory or scout your next opponent and simply say, "Score more goals than the other team next game," or "That was entertaining" and be done. That's crazy! You are looking for themes, your game-plan, and your team identity in your play and that of your opponents to gain an advantage or tap into an idea or strategy that will bring about success and victory. You get specific, focus on tendencies, and you look for ways your strengths can be maximized and how you can take advantage of your opponents' weaknesses.

The same is true for life as you compete and life after playing. Your life themes are specifics, indicators, and tendencies that continue to show up in and bring out passion and joy in your life. So, take some time to reflect, watch some *film* of your life and remember those moments when passion overflowed. My hope is you identify those passions and zero in on them within your sport to clarify those life themes and take those themes into whatever career you step into next.

As I continued to watch the *film* of my life, another theme I observed was *gatherer of people.* I am an extrovert and love to be around people, but there was something else beyond being around people that continued to pop up in my life. I would see those on the outskirts of the team. I saw the teammate who wasn't included, the player who would linger outside of the main circle, and those who were shy or kept to themselves. I would work to engage with them and connect them to the team and group. The funny thing is that I have taken numerous personality and strength tests over the years, and all of them point to this life theme. In each test, there was a component of including, gathering, and incorporating people into whatever team I was leading, competing against, or building. Not only was it a strength, but I was passionate about it, and when someone who was on the outside was invited into the group, that brought joy to my soul.

I want to take a brief moment to remind and emphasize the importance that life is about more than just you. Your why and your life themes will continually point outside of yourself, and your why will take you beyond simply personal gain or fulfillment. When you are at your best, moving toward your true north, it is not about you. If you decide to make it all about yourself, your why, and how you express your passion, you will limit and cap your impact and success. You will also be left with feelings of emptiness and loneliness. Humans are meant to live within communities and engage with others. I don't know how many times I have heard post-retirement professional athletes talk about the locker room and that the relationships they developed are what they miss the most. We are at our best when we express our why, passions, and life themes outwardly with and to others.

3. Create and write a personal mission statement.

When I was growing up in Michigan, we would go camping throughout the year. My earlier memories of camping were with my dad, who would take me out into our yard to camp in a tent. Sometimes we would simply sleep under the stars. As I grew up, my father gave me a compass for the camping and hiking trips when he wasn't with me. One of the first things I learned when I started camping with my dad, other than building a fire, was how to read a compass. The compass helped guide and direct where I was going, wanted to go, or return back to where we set up camp. Even if I got off track wandering through the woods, the compass would guide me back to where I needed to be to get back to camp or find where we parked the car.

Another way to think about finding your direction and staying on course can also be seen in the sky. I now live in a city with lights all around, but when we went camping, the only light even close was from the fire and our flashlights. The night sky was illuminated with stars far more than I could ever count. Even though it was fun to try and count all of the stars in the night sky, the stars also served as a map and guide for those who traveled at night. Early in history, sailors and travelers would use the night sky to guide themselves and even tell time by tracking groupings of stars called constellations, with Polaris, or the North Star, front and center. These groupings of stars were named by people who thought the star groupings looked like objects, people, and animals. Polaris is part of the constellation called Ursa Major. Another constellation is Orion and his belt. Other than the north star's use for directional purposes while traveling, I was curious if there were other purposes for the constellations.

Thank you, Google. I searched "purpose for star constellations."[5] There was plenty of links to answer my question. The main purpose was directional. When disoriented, lost, or in need of direction, on the ocean especially, people would look up at the night sky and be able to figure out where they were, clarify their directional heading, and adjust their path to make sure they were pointed in the right direction. Constellations were also used for mapping out the night sky and giving some order to all of those bright lights up there. They were also used for agriculture. Based on when specific constellations appeared and their location in the night sky, people would plant their crops and harvest them.

Map Out Your Mission

A mission statement is similar to creating a map or directional setting for your life that is tied to your values. Your mission statement will act in much the same way as a compass or constellations in the night sky. Life doesn't always go as planned, and there are moments when things go sideways, or obstacles and setbacks come your way. You can get placed on a completely different path due to decisions or circumstances completely out of your control. Look at 2020!

Your personal mission statement will help guide, map out, realign, and remind you of your true north, give clarity on where you are, and point you back in the direction you want to go. Your life themes are like guard rails on a highway that make the most of your passions, talents, desires, and personality but keep you on track going in the direction of your *north star*. And by writing out your mission statement, you are clarifying your *north star* that will point you in the direction your heart desires to go.

Andy Andrews, *New York Times* best-selling author, writes about five questions everyone must answer when you write out your personal mission statement.[6]

1. What is important to you? This is looking at your values.
2. Where do you want to go? This refers to personal accomplishments, where you see yourself in the future, how do you want your life to look physically, emotionally, spiritually, and mentally.
3. What does *the best* look like for me? Describe what the best looks like for you, and dream about your best possible results.
4. How do you want to act? What's your character like? How would people describe you? How would you desire people to describe you?
5. What kind of legacy do I want to leave behind? Fifty years from now, what does the impact of your life look like? How will you be remembered? How will those whom you impact be influencing and changing sport, neighborhoods, and our world?

After answering those questions, here are guidelines to help you write out your personal mission statement.

*   Keep it simple and short so you can memorize it. Don't overcomplicate it. My dad would remind me all the time when I was growing up to keep things simple; the more complicated it gets, the harder it will become to remember.

- Include your values, passions, and dreams.
- List what you care about. What are issues or problems to which you want to be or find a solution?
- Know your personality traits, skills, and abilities. Know how you function at your best and clarify how will you stay in that space as often as possible.
- Finally, it's okay to make changes and adjustments along the way.

My personal mission statement is to "live to be at my best so I can assist others to do the same."

Follow the Direction of Your Life Theme

Your *Life Themes* comprise the consistencies within your story, what inspires you, and your personal mission statement. When you examine these, you will begin to see your themes clarified and rise to the top. When silver is refined, the dross, or waste, rises to the top, and you are able to skim it away, leaving the precious metal in its pure form. That is what you are doing as you identify your *Life Themes*. You are growing in your self-awareness and intentionally refining yourself to be at your best. You are giving yourself direction and building a map to live out who you are and what you do when you are at your best.

I shared earlier glimpses of my *Life Themes* in this chapter. As I took a closer look at my own life, three themes have continued to pop up in my sport and competition, relationships, actions, and thought processes. My *Life Themes* are educator and coach, gatherer of people, and overcoming.

When I look back at my life, I first recognize the educator and coach and gatherer themes when I was

in middle school. I remember desiring to get everyone involved in sport, activities, and even within the
classroom. I felt drawn to those on the fringe and was
compelled to bring them into the group. The theme of
overcoming became clearer when I began to reflect on
my story and remember those moments that shaped my
life. I realized I had experienced obstacles, setbacks, and
uncontrollable negative circumstances, yet I was able to
overcome them to get where I am today.

Knowing your Life Themes gives you clarity, strength,
and reassurance. It is like having a map that not only
points you in a direction but also clarifies the path and
destination. The next time you look up at the night sky,
remember those are not only lights in the night; stars
represent direction, history, road map, and life for many,
and your Life Themes will guide you much the same!

PART 3
IMAGINE THE FUTURE

Where there is no vision, the people perish.

—ancient proverb[7]

I remember, at seven years old, standing in my bedroom in front of a mirror watching myself practice athletic moves that I had seen the day before on TV. Growing up, I was told that God knew all things, so I thought, "If God is watching me right now, could I fake Him out?" I didn't know, but I knew I was going to try because if I could juke God, I could juke anyone! I would fake a run to the left but then go right and vice versa; I would even throw in some double, triple and even quadruple fakes to test the waters. I'm not sure if it ever worked, but it's a funny memory of my seven-year-old self.

The other thing I would do was imagine myself as a running back for the Detroit Lions, faking players out left and right. I would stand there seeing myself out on the football field. I would run in place and see linebackers coming at me, and I would fake one way and go the other. Or I would do a double fake—fake left, fake right, and then run left. Before Barry Sanders (still the best running back of all time, in my opinion) was doing his thing on the football field, the Detroit Lions had a running back named Billy Sims, who also wore the #20 jersey. As I look back, it's funny to think about a skinny little red-headed kid in his underwear (did I forget to mention that?) imagining himself in a Detroit Lions #20 jersey trying to juke, fake, and spin move my way to a touchdown.

There is something to imagining yourself doing great things. Our imaginations are powerful, and using imagery builds innovation and creativity. I still laugh at those memories, but the irony is I was practicing something powerful that impacted my thought process, mentality, and athleticism. When I would go out and play pick-up football or on the soccer field, I would do those moves I imagined myself doing and practicing in my bedroom. A little juke, a slight feint, fake right, then go left. There is something to the action and practice of visualization that transfers to actionable results.

When you imagine the future, you are taking steps to envision yourself in those spaces. As an athlete, how many times have you dreamed of holding the championship trophy? How often have you pretended to be at-bat in the bottom of the ninth inning, two outs, runner on first, and down by one, only to hit the game-winning home run? Have you thought about what it would feel like to have confetti fall down on your head after winning the national championship or standing on the podium and bowing as someone places the medal around your neck at the Olympics?

There is power in imagining, and that is what you are going to do in this next step in SHIFT, *Imagine the*

Future. You are going to journey to the future and begin to envision and dream about what could be. You will identify and picture what will be that trophy holding moment in your sport and within your life. Time to dream!

CHAPTER 7

HOW WILL YOU DREAM WITH PURPOSE AND ACTION?

Action without vision is only passing time,
vision without action is merely daydreaming,
but vision with action can change the world.

— Joel A. Barker

Have you ever climbed up a ladder? Once you lean it up against a wall or a tree or the side of a building, you start to climb it to reach the area you were unable to reach from the ground. Think about the ladder as your life. You are climbing and working toward something that is high above you that you can see but are unable to reach. You climb and climb, but what happens as you climb up life's ladder is that you start getting close to the top, then arrive only to realize you leaned it against the wrong building.

As athletes, there are a lot of times when you are told what to do, when to do it, and for how long. Your time, schedule, trainings, and calendar are set for you—even when you break things down into one season. At the beginning of a season, the goal is to play in the championship game and win. Having a clear idea, a destination in mind, gives purpose and meaning to what you do each day. There is familiarity to the rhythm, and as you continue moving forward in that season and beyond, have you ever stopped to look around and see where you are at or the direction you are going?

Sport and life have a number of similarities. As you start moving in a direction and get familiar with the rhythm, you keep going with the flow and direction you are moving. Then, you are climbing the ladder, and the person holding the ladder makes you get off, or worse, pulls you off. Your entire life has been focused in on climbing this ladder and reaching the top. Now, you are told to get off. As you stand there staring at the ladder, wishing and desiring you were back on it, it's gone, and you are left to find another ladder on your own.

"After climbing a great hill, one only finds that there are many more hills to climb."
— Nelson Mandela

One of the more difficult realities athletes must face is that the ladder they are climbing is only one of many ladders in their life. Simply because you retire, graduate, or have a career-ending injury doesn't mean your life is over; it merely means there is another ladder you will need to start climbing. Nelson Mandela said, "After climbing a great hill (ladder), one only finds that there are many more hills (ladders) to climb." There is truth in his words, but it doesn't make things any easier!

Your entire life, you have focused on climbing this ladder called sport, and you have made it to the top or at least closer to the top, and the view is nice! Then it's gone, taken from you, and you are told you must start over within another arena. The harsh reality of professional sport is that very few athletes get to choose that moment when they leave the game. Very few will actually get an article or interview on ESPN or the league website making the announcement. Then you are left to your own thoughts and ideas, standing there wishing you were back on that ladder and still climbing.

Start Again

We love board games in our family, and this love started early in the lives of my girls. One game that was particularly frustrating for me on so many different levels was Chutes and Ladders. The premise of the game is that each player takes a turn by spinning the spinner. Whatever number you get is the number of spaces you move on the board. On the board, there are 100 spaces, and on many of the spaces, there is either a chute or a ladder. Depending on which space you landed on, you will either climb a ladder or slide down and go backwards on a chute.

There was this one space that was particularly frustrating. It would send you down about fifty spaces; it was awful. What it would truly do was prolong the game much more than it needed to be. You could be winning, and then all of a sudden, you would spin and move your piece, and there you go down the chute fifty spaces. My daughter would always laugh at my misfortune. The chute took you close to the beginning of the game board, so you were basically starting over. Did I mention this game was very frustrating?

Whenever that day comes when you hang up your shoes for the last time, take your last walk back into the locker room, or jog out onto the field for the last time, so many emotions fill your mind and body. You are being knocked off the ladder you have climbed your entire life, and you are starting over. You go from thousands cheering your name to the beginner beside other people who are getting started. It is never easy to start over or be an amateur again.

It is like hitting that chute that knocks you back fifty spaces, but it's okay. Anything worth doing is worth doing well. Even though you are still young, it can feel daunting knowing you are back in that status of being a rookie or freshman again. You may experience frustration, nerves, fear, feel demeaned, and a whole lot of other emotions, but here is a secret—it's okay. It is okay to feel that way and to grapple with the reality that you will never again put on the jersey.

Acknowledge That Change Is Coming

The first step in Imagining the Future is the acknowledgment.

When you acknowledge that your career will come to an end eventually, it is easier to begin to envision what life could possibly look like after sport. You may be saying, "Jonathan, I know it will come to an end, but I will take care of that whenever it gets here."

In high school, I ran in the 4x400 meter relay race. Within this race and other relays, there are small yet significant moments in the race, namely the handoffs between the runners. In that short, quick moment of transition when one runner hands off the baton to the next runner is when you are either standing on the podium or looking up at it. I remember spending hours working on these transition moments, focused on the timing and steps within the handoff zone.

At the 2008 Beijing Olympic Games, both the men's and women's 4x400 relay teams for the USA were highly touted and expected to stand on the podium. Neither team even qualified for the finals because they either missed the handoff or dropped the baton. The expectation for those teams was gold medals and hearing the Star-Spangled Banner playing in the stadium. The women missed the finals for the first time in sixty years, and the men had only missed twice in nearly one hundred years![8]

The chief executive officer of USA Track and Field was quoted after the two races saying that there would be "a comprehensive review" and "included in this assessment . . . will be the way we select, train and coach our relays." There was disappointment, anger, frustration, shame, and guilt because of not measuring up to the expectation. Transitions are not guaranteed to be easy or handed to you. Even if you are the best or at the top of your sport, transitions can still make or break you.

Don't push aside or hit the pause button on preparing for these transitions, however small or significant. Especially don't ignore the transition, whenever that day may come, where you close the door on your athletic career. Acknowledge it and begin to prepare now for it.

Adjust Your Perspective of Change

The second step to Imagining the Future is adjusting your perspective of change.

While you don't know exactly when those moments of transition will occur in sport, you do know they are coming and will occur whether or not you are ready. So you'd better be prepared. Benjamin Franklin said, "If you fail to plan, you are planning to fail." That is true for sport, life, and your life after playing. The transition will come at some point; simply because you don't see or know the moment when your career will come to an end doesn't mean you shouldn't take the time to prepare for it.

When you think about retirement, you think of being sixty-five and receiving social security. As an elite athlete, your retirement from the sport occurs in your late twenties or mid-thirties. Now, if you are one of the lucky few who get to play their sport into their late thirties or early forties, bravo to you. Again, you are talking about a tiny fraction of 1 percent. So few athletes have that choice or get that opportunity. The idea of retiring from your sport at thirty with so much of your life ahead of you and more questions than answers can be daunting. Whether you have questions about finances, what will you do for work, what your legacy as an athlete will be, how will you provide for your family, and a myriad of other questions, doesn't it make sense to prepare for your life after playing?

As an athlete, you have had to pivot, change, and make adjustments athletically countless times. How many changes or shifts or adjustments do you make in a game? There are probably some data analytics about this somewhere. The point is that you make adjustments, but your game plan or strategy is still the same. Even if your strategy or game isn't working, you change that. But here is the kicker; you have planned for it! You have prepared for those moments where you may or may not have to change or adjust your game plan and strategy to find success.

You can't predict the future, nor can a crystal ball tell you what your life will look like five years from now. It's almost impossible to look ahead and know exactly when you will stop competing. Maybe you are at the beginning of your pro career, and life is good. Perhaps you are at the tail end and getting ready to sign your last contract, or you are done playing, or somewhere in the middle. Sport and life are unpredictable, and one of the keys to being successful in both is preparation. As you begin to dream and think about what's next, preparation is essential.

How you leave one arena or space directly affects how you enter the next. I have never met an athlete who said they desired not to be successful or wanted to fail at whatever they do in sport and life. You desire success, but success starts with the first step. Preparation is at the beginning of your journey, so you have to start to prepare now to be successful for whenever that transition occurs. Start thinking and planning for your future today. It doesn't have to involve a great deal of time or energy either, but you do need to start.

Four Tips on Changing Your Perspective

I remember the first time I heard about compound interest in financial investments. The premise is that as you invest your money, the interest you gain over time builds on itself and drastically increases the value of your investment. The longer you have to invest, the greater the value will be. The same idea is true for the transition to life after playing. If you only start preparing once you are done competing, you will not have much to work with, and the pressure to figure it out will be high. If you start early to prepare for life after playing, beginning by imagining what life after playing could be, and you start investing small amounts early on in your career, then whenever that day may come, you will be prepared to make the transition because you have invested in yourself and your life after playing.

Again, preparation doesn't mean you are focusing all of your time on what's your next career. Start by making small investments, and those investments will build over time. You will need to change your perspective about life after sport and the transitions you will experience as an athlete and beyond. To help you get started making this adjustment of your perspective on change, here is a four-step exercise to get you thinking and preparing for what life after sport could look like.

1. **Dream**—What do you want in life after sport? Do you want to be your own boss? Set your own schedule? Is there a specific industry or space in which you want to work? Action: Write out three to four sentences describing your ideal situation.

2. **Discuss (Invite or Share)**—You don't need to tell everyone, but you do need to tell someone. Initiate a conversation with a close friend, family, or mentor. By discussing your dream, you are giving yourself the opportunity for accountability, to ask questions, gain outside perspective, and get clarity.

3. **Modify (Revise or Adapt)**—When you are imagining the future, it is merely that—the future—so you can't do nothing and expect a clear prediction. Things change, shift, and move, and it's okay to adjust your dream and clarify what you are pursuing as time moves forward. You make adjustments as the season goes on as

a player and team. You will also need to make adjustments along the way to your dream, and that's okay!

4. **Assess (Evaluate)**—How are you doing as you move closer to the next phase of life? Are you moving yourself closer to what your dream envisions? Are you working toward that vision and putting yourself in the best possible position for whenever that day comes?

Picture It

The third key to Imagining the Future is to picture it.

I don't know about you, but I am a huge believer in visualization! The art of sitting quietly and picturing yourself acting, responding, and competing the way you desire to act, respond, or compete. What that means is visually picturing what it looks like for you to be at your best in a game, at your job, within your relationships, or speaking.

I was first introduced to the idea and practice of visualization when I was at Ohio Wesleyan University. I was talking with the head coach, Dr. Jay Martin, and he encouraged me to start visualizing what I wanted to happen in the games, specifically in key moments. So, I started with the kick-off and the first five minutes, and I visualized how to start strong and set the tone of the match. I was a defensive midfielder, a six. One of the components and roles I played was to set the tone early in a game. It could be a tackle, an intercepted pass, a 50-50 ball, or a counterattack with a pass that started our offensive movement forward. What's interesting is that each of those plays is a moment of transition in the game. They are small moments that could possibly lead to scoring a goal, but that wasn't necessarily the objective. The focus was to set the tone, grab momentum, and take it to your opponent. So, after practice a few days a week, I would sit and visualize the first five minutes of a game. I spent time going through the different scenarios of how I could maximize the first five minutes. I would clearly visualize the things I wanted to do, how I would navigate a counterattack, see myself winning 50-50 balls, or setting up the offensive movement forward.

I would also envision specific moments of playing at my best and replay those moments over and over in my head. One thing Jay would also tell me was to engage as many of my senses as possible. I imagined as much detail as possible when visualizing those moments. To increase or add to my visualization, I would sit in the stadium while I did it. Sitting in the stadium would allow me to engage my senses of smell and sound directly. I could smell what was in the air and hear the noises around the stadium. It brought the visualization to life, engaged the motor memory I was building, and strengthened my motor memory, so when those moments occurred in the game, my brain would say, "I have been here before. I know what to do. I have seen this." I would then be able to respond proactively in the moment.

It may seem simple, but the reality is most of sport and life is simple. That doesn't make it easy. This third key is simple, but it can be difficult to be patient and visualize what life after sport could look like and what new arena you want to be playing in, especially when you want only to focus on your sport and what you are doing in the moment. But take the time to visualize and picture your future!

Take Ownership of Your Story

I am writing this book during the pandemic in 2020 of COVID 19, and it has affected the entire world. If nothing else, COVID 19 has shown us there is more to life than sport, money, and fame. So much in our world has been halted, paused, removed, or masked. As I write these words, there have been multiple professional athletes opting out of competing in the fall. They are leaving millions of dollars on the table to take a year off. Why?

There are multiple reasons why, and answers are different for every athlete. One overarching reality is about the future and what the future holds for athletes and for sport. You have one chance to write your story, and if you don't write it, someone else will. That's what I want to encourage you to realize; if you are not writing your own story, if you are not imagining the future for where you'll be, then someone else is going to do it for you. My hope is that you take ownership of your life, write your story, and maximize your power to impact the space you live in!

I was recently talking with professional cyclist Ben King about the transition to life after sport. He has been cycling professionally for ten years. I asked him what advice he would give his younger self if he could go back and have that conversation. He said to "trust the process and listen to your coaches." When you are first starting up as a professional, you are excited about what's ahead of you. You have visions of grandeur, winning trophies, and being the best, and the thought or idea of something beyond that seems crazy. You don't have to figure everything out right away. Simply take steps forward, and trust the process. This book is taking you through a process to dream about the future and prepare for life after sport; trust the process.

Three guides to help you imagine the future:

1. *Be present and engaged in the moment.* When you are with others, put your phone away, and engage relationally with those around you. Make yourself known as you intentionally get to know those on your team. Be curious! You are an elite athlete, and you have experienced the world and have interesting stories and things to share. Don't hide behind your screen or be distant. Being present invites you to engage and be yourself.

2. *Celebrate the small victories.* As you are working through *Imagining the Future*, you will have moments and milestones when you take strides forward. Go out for a special dinner, make a memory, or do something special to celebrate and make sure to bring those in your team along with you.

3. *Look back occasionally to see how far you have come.* It's like looking at the flight plan when you are traveling. On the screens on the back of the seats in front of you, there is an option to see the flight plan. There is an airplane on the map showing you where you are, where your departure city was located, and where you are going (your arrival city). It even has the temperature outside the plane, your speed, the time you left, and the time you will arrive at your destination. When you look back occasionally, it affords you the opportunity to celebrate how far you have

gone. When we push through and grind it out through a season, we are so focused on what's ahead that we forget to look back to see how far we have come. So, look back occasionally and celebrate.

Life isn't over when you finish competing; it means you get the opportunity to start climbing a new ladder. You have a strong foundation for who you are and the story you are writing as you adjust your perspective and picture the future. Anatole Frank said, "To accomplish great things we must not only act but also dream, not only plan, but also believe." You are the only you in our world, so make the most of who you are, what you can accomplish in this world, and the impact you can have around you. Life is greater than your sport. You have the choice today to dream and believe about what's next and how you will live now and as you *Imagine the Future*.

CHAPTER 8

HAVE YOU EVER BUILT A MAP WITHOUT A DESTINATION?

If you don't know where you are going, you'll
end up someplace else.

—Yogi Berra

Pirate Captain Jack Sparrow, made famous through the
Pirates of the Caribbean movies, encountered many obstacles throughout his journeys. In *Pirates of the Caribbean:
Dead Man's Chest*, Captain Jack has a magical compass
that at first glance appears to be broken. It doesn't point
toward north and changes the direction it points as
different people handle and use it. At one point in the
movie, the value of the compass is revealed when Lord
Cutler Beckett, chairman of the East India Trading
Company, sends Will Turner to retrieve or steal it from
Captain Jack Sparrow. The leader of the trading company says the compass points toward that which you

most desire. The magical compass sets the direction and course for whatever your heart desires the most. Wouldn't that be amazing to have in our own lives? Perhaps not, but the premise of the magical compass has importance for us today because we all have hearts' desires, dreams, and aspirations. So, what is your heart's desire? What do you value and desire to go after? What do you want your future to look like, and where do you want to go and achieve?

Championships, trophies, winning your last game—these are all dreams that individuals and teams are striving for each season! There is a clear destination in mind when the season begins. Each year, there is a time the team sits down and writes out the goals for the season. I don't think I have ever been on a team that didn't want to win the championship or be champions of the league. There was a clear destination that you, individually and as a team, were all working and striving toward. The destination was set!

Journey or Destination?

There is debate or at least a fun conversation about which is more important—the journey or the destination. For me, it's a trick question because there is power and necessity for both. You must have a clear destination or target to aim at, but you also need to focus on the present, the journey you are on today. Enjoy the moments, this present, this gift that is in front of you—don't miss it. Even when you are in those difficult times, the messy middle, when you are grinding out through the summer heat, a down-spell in performance, losing streak, or struggles in relationships—be present in the journey. There is much to learn and grow from while in the heat of the battle!

As you *Imagine the Future*, you are creating a map with a direction heading to help guide you forward. You will need a direction to move. The power of a map isn't only to help you see where you are, but also where you want to go. It points you in the direction of that which you desire most in life, just as the magic compass did for Captain Jack Sparrow.

The intentionality of clarifying and knowing your identity, your story, your why, your personal values, and your life themes is not for those to be out on their own. Rather, all of what you have navigated, processed through, clarified, and identified is to be used, filtered through, and overlapped as you imagine the future and build your life map.

That which you most desire to see, accomplish, and pursue now, as well as into the future, flows through those other aspects, filters, and life perspectives. Think about it this way. Have you ever walked at night or in a dark space with a flashlight? It is pretty cool what occurs. The flashlight sends out this beam of light and illuminates whatever you point it at. What's amazing is that the beam only illuminates that which is in its path. There are plenty of other objects, people, and things within the area or space; however, the only things you are able to see are what the flashlight is pointed at in that moment. So what are you illuminating? Where is your flashlight pointing, and what do you see?

Don't Get Distracted

I remember one of the first times I went camping with friends. We snuck into a local state park because we wanted to camp along the Chippewa River. You were not allowed to stay overnight, so we got dropped off about forty-five minutes before the park closed after the rangers made their rounds to make sure no one was left in the park. We hiked quickly through a field and had to use our flashlights as we got to the wooded area. By the time we made it to the river, it was night and dark. The only things we could see was what we pointed our flashlights at. We knew there was plenty of vegetation and wildlife around us; we couldn't see it. We could hear animals walking through the woods as they neared the river, but we couldn't see them. It was a bit eerie hearing the footsteps, but because our view and sight were limited, we couldn't see the animals.

When you imagine the future, you are illuminating the target area or space you would like to go. There are a number of things out there that you can't control as you

> "You will never reach your destination if you stop and throw stones at every dog that barks."
> —Winston Churchill

start working toward your target. If we had moved our flashlights all around and never focused on the direction we were headed, we could have moved forward, but it would have taken drastically longer. By focusing on an area and illuminating it, basically dreaming about what the future could look like, you will begin to see it. You will create an idea, an image of the future and start moving in that direction and exploring. When you begin thinking about the future, there are a lot of distractions around you—pressure to perform, family dynamics, frustrations with your agent or current club situation, and a myriad of other things vying for your attention. I love what Winston Churchill said about the distractions around us: "You will never reach your destination if you stop and throw stones at every dog that barks." There are "dogs" in you and around your life that are barking. Don't allow them to distract you and keep you from pursuing your destination.

The Adventure Continues

As an elite athlete, you have taken the time to prepare, develop, and grow. Each season you prepare physically, mentally, intellectually, and emotionally for the season ahead as well as maintaining that growth throughout the season. You had an image of what you desired to accomplish by the end of the season. You had a championship, a record, distance, desired outcomes, goals, milestones, etc., that you desired to achieve, so you imagined it! What's holding you back from intentionally preparing and imagining what you want for your life after playing? Why not begin to prepare for whatever your next career or venture will be and transition well whenever that day may come? You don't have to wait. Start imagining today!

Before you even begin to object with a long list of why you don't want to start imagining, let's hit pause! There isn't an athlete out there who doesn't know his or her career will come to an end at some point. That might seem obvious, but the reality is that it is difficult to think about and imagine the future. The thought of pursuing something other than your sport probably hasn't come across your mind much as you are intensely focused on your sport, your performance, and what you desire to achieve. Maybe you have thought about life after playing, but it's overwhelming. Where do you even begin? Perhaps you may be in a situation where it is taboo or unprofessional to talk about anything other than your sport because it is seen or viewed as a weakness or you not being committed.

Regardless of where you are, you have to start somewhere. You have taken the time, energy, and effort to explore and know who you are, what drives you, and what makes you tick. Now, it's time to think about what that next step could be and your direction. As an elite athlete, you are in such a difficult reality. You have focused on your sport for around twenty years and have spent countless hours zeroing in on your craft. Now, at an age where most others are starting their careers, you are ending yours and looking to start over in a completely new career. The reality is heavy and tough to process and think about.

You have time to dream and think about what you are passionate about and how you could take that passion and make it a vocation, a career, or even simply explore a new arena. You now have the opportunity not only to play a game and get paid, but you now get to think about the next career, opportunity beyond your sport, and prepare for it.

Life is an adventure, and if it was only a straight line from point A to point B, it wouldn't be that enjoyable. You have the opportunity to live fully now and in whatever your next career may be, so why not take the time to dream about it and take some action toward that next step?

Where Are You Headed?

"What does the future hold?" is one of those questions that athletes and people alike have been asking for generations! But why not take the initiative with your future and the unknown that comes with it. You have a choice to clarify and aim at something. Pick a new arena to compete in, seek out opportunities, and dip your toes into something new. You may surprise yourself with what you discover. What's freeing as you take this initiative is that you are not fixed into that decision or future for the rest of your life. So, discover and explore. If you never aim at the target, you will never hit it. Hockey great Wayne Gretzky said it well. "You will miss 100% of the shots you never take." So, take a shot. Go for it!

Choose something to pursue, and if, for some reason, it isn't a good fit for you, that's okay. What is important is choosing a destination. It gives you something to shoot toward, a target to aim at. Chinese philosopher and educator, Confucius, warns about the struggle of not making a choice, "He who chases two rabbits, catches none." Choose an industry, a specific vocation, an arena to explore, or even a specific job; choose something and go after it.

Picture yourself sitting in your car. You are in the driver's seat, getting ready to go somewhere. As you prepare to turn the key or push the start button, you take a few short actions; check your mirrors, buckle your seat belt, and look around for other vehicles. Your side mirrors, rearview mirror, and the windshield in front of you all help you navigate to your destination. When you are driving, you are focused forward and driving toward a location. You have a target in mind, and you are taking turns and maneuvering toward that location. You have identified it, maybe even plugged it into your maps app, and you begin the journey toward it.

While in the car, you use those mirrors and windows to help you navigate, change lanes, make turns, and most importantly, see what's ahead of you. There is a reason the windshield is the biggest of all the windows. The side mirrors help you see what's around you. The rearview mirror helps you see what's behind you. The windshield helps you see where you are going and what's directly in front of you.

Life and sport are often like driving. In sport, you see what's around you, and in some sports like basketball, football, and soccer, having good vision is essential for success. As you *Imagine the Future*, you are working on your vision and focusing on what's ahead. You utilize your personal *mirrors*, your identity, your story, your experience, your values, and your life themes—what we have already explored and identified earlier in this book. Those are your side mirrors, rearview mirror, your engine, and your fuel. They help guide and direct and move you, but you must look forward to grow, develop, find success, and reach your destination.

It may seem obvious, but it is imperative that your eyes are open while you drive. It is never safe to keep your eyes closed while driving! Bringing clarity to your life gives you peace, confidence, and strength. There's a sense of knowing where you are going, the destination, and the next step, and as you move forward toward being and competing as your best self, to put your best foot forward. We want to continue to bring clarity to our vision by bringing into focus what's in front of you and help you bring clarity to your vision by having your eyes open now and as you imagine the future.

One of the most powerful aspects of Google Maps or Apple Maps on your mobile device is that it not only has all of these destinations built into it but, most importantly, when you identify the destination you desire to go, it gives you a step by step plan to get there. Unfortunately, life isn't quite that easy, but the same premise holds true. Unless you pick a destination, you will never get there. There are millions of destinations, places to go and experience, and that is the beauty of being human and having a choice, but you still have to choose, or someone else will make the choice for you. If you allow others to make the choice, you will aimlessly drift through this life, ebbing and flowing with whatever whim or person moves you.

It's Your Choice

You have chosen your sport to compete in, that was a destination, and you have been amazingly successful at it. Eventually, you will have to move onto something else. Why not be ready for that moment and have a destination in mind? I remember talking to Mike, a professional soccer player, who loved chess. I am more of a checkers guy, but when we were playing, I asked him what he enjoyed about the game. He said it was that you had to think multiple steps ahead of where you were on the board to be successful. There was this simultaneous thought process of being in the present, yet also thinking five, ten, or fifteen steps ahead of where you were.

How will you *Imagine the Future*? Will you let it merely happen and give your power and ability to choose to someone else, or will you take the time to think about who you are and how you are created and wired and pick a destination? What do the next steps in your life look like? Choose today to *Imagine the Future* and take the first step!

CHAPTER 9
DON'T GO ALONE: HOW BUILDING A TEAM WILL TAKE YOU FURTHER

To go fast go alone, to go far go together.

—African proverb

Have you ever watched or been to an awards celebration? I always enjoy hearing what the athletes have to say in response to the award they have won. It gives the listeners a glimpse into the soul of the individual—how they talk about themselves, view themselves or others, and what they have accomplished.

What usually stands out to me within these speeches are the people the athlete thanks. It is interesting to me who they choose and why. I wish there was an opportunity to ask follow up questions or the athlete had more time to explain why they choose each individual. One can deduce a parent or maybe the coach who gave them their first opportunity, but more often than not, there are others—grandparents, aunts or uncles, other coaches or trainers, the occasional friend or teammate, and every once in a while, someone is mentioned who comes so far out of nowhere that the crowd is left wondering, "Who is that?"

Regardless of who is mentioned or celebrated during these speeches and ceremonies, the reality is no one has ever achieved their success on their own. The old adage of "it takes a village" is so true. To help propel one individual toward athletic, community, business, or academic success takes a group of others that surround the one; they encourage, celebrate, sacrifice, challenge, and push the one so they can find success. You stand on the shoulders of those who have come before you, and they are continually holding you up.

Who Speaks Into Your Life?

There are a few limitations in life and our personal relationships. First is your immediate family; you are stuck with them whether you like it or not. You can't change your parents or your siblings if you have them, extended family, aunts, uncles, grandparents; they are your family, and you can't change that fact. You have a choice on who you allow into your life. You have the ability to choose your friends, confidantes, coaches, trusted advisors, and whether or not you allow certain family members access to your life.

But here's a question for you: Have you ever thought about what should characterize those you allow to speak into your life? It may seem weird or a little funny to ask that question, but when you are so focused on your sport, performance, and striving toward your athletic or business goals, wouldn't it make sense to have those around you have a character that is trustworthy, humble, and honoring to you? Shouldn't those around you desire to help you move your career, endeavors, and your life forward?

As an athlete, you are scrutinized, analyzed, and critiqued on how well you perform and what results you are producing. Now, I know it may seem difficult to quantify character, but you can experience and observe it. Like a skilled coach looking to add to her roster, you have the opportunity to build your own team.

Coaches go over film, talk to scouts, other coaches or directors, managers, and even family and childhood friends to get an idea about the individual athlete they are recruiting or looking to sign to a contract. Long hours and hard work are put into identifying the right players for the right positions at the right time to give the team its greatest opportunity for success. Talent is the obvious trait that coaches look for, but it is what's below the surface—their character—that sets athletes and people apart from others.

So, let's take some time and look below the surface with your life and those you have invited into your inner circle. Jim Rohn has been attributed to saying, "You're the average of the five people you spend the most time with." There is a variation of that quote that says, "Show me your friends, and I'll show you your future." What does that say about you and your future? If you took the five closest people around you and averaged them, what would you discover about yourself? The people with whom you surround yourself directly affect the person you will become—how you will act, your character and mindset development, and your growth path.

> "Show me your friends, and I'll show you your future."
> — Unknown

Let's put your coaching hat on and begin to put your team together. In sport, you fill out positions, skill sets, character, leadership, experience, and a few other specifics that fit you as a coach, like playing style or formation preference. The first thing a coach does is take an honest look at the current roster and then begin to decide the areas that are needed to find success at the next level. So, take an honest look at the five people you spend the most time with, whether talking on the phone, in person, who you seek out advice, etc. Do they reflect who you desire to be? Do they have your best interest in mind when it comes to where you desire to go athletically and in life? As a coach, who would be the ideal teammate for your players and for yourself? What qualities, personalities, attitudes, mentalities, and experiences would you be looking for to build your team?

Who are the people that you desire to make up your *team* when you are imagining the future and think about what's next for your life in the next season or even after your playing career finishes? When you dream and think about the future, who do you want to be there with you, experiencing those moments by your side as you go after that a dream, desire, or a goal?

Let's get started; it's time to build your team!

Find People Who Share a Common Purpose

You can only go as far as your own legs will take you. That seems obvious, but something happens in your mind and within your body when you are pushed to the limits in the company of other people. There is an extra boost that you receive internally when you know someone else is in the fight with you. You can train harder, go further, and push beyond your perceived boundaries when you know someone else is there beside you doing the same thing and going after the same goals and dreams.

When you have someone next to you, it enables you to tap into something that you didn't yet realize you possessed or could achieve. In sport, there is always someone else who has pushed, encouraged, helped, challenged, ignited, or believed in you; that is how you have achieved as much as you have. Even in individual sports, there has always been someone else in your corner.

Knowing there has always been someone championing you through your sport only reveals how imperative it is to identify and lock arms with others while you *Imagine the Future*. Knowing you will have someone else journeying with you gives you courage, strength, and the ability to do things or go after dreams that, on your own strength, you didn't know you could pursue. Having someone journeying alongside you gives you the fortitude and strength to dream and go after a future that seems so far off, similar to your athletic dreams and how coaches, teammates, parents, friends joined with you to help you get to where you wanted to go.

Coaches and scouts spend years honing their craft to identify the right and best talent to fit the philosophy, tactics, character, leadership, and personalities of their teams. Now that you are focusing in on building your team, how do you identify people you want with you as you get started? How will you figure out who you want to journey alongside you? These are good questions to ask yourself because it is not as easy as you may think, but it is not as complex either.

Start simple with those who are already around you. These are the people immediately connected to you and who have journeyed alongside you up until this moment and who have helped you get to where you are today.

The first step might seem obvious when you begin to *Imagine the Future*; who are those currently speaking and building into your life? Bring this select group of people with you as you think about and dream about what could be next. Remember, the African proverb is true. "To go fast, go alone, to go far, go together." So, identify those select few who are currently surrounding and journeying alongside you.

After acknowledging who is already speaking into your life, start to think about those outside of your immediate circle. Who would you want to be a part of what you are doing and where you are going? You can't have everyone, but you do want to be specific and intentional. This isn't a small decision to make. It's important, and you want to be intentional about it.

Think like a manager for a moment as you put your team together. Who are the *players* you want on your team? Think of the speeches at those award ceremonies. Think about who you would honor that has helped you along your journey. What were their characteristics that inspired you and motivated you to succeed? Talking about the power of a common goal, purpose and direction, Jim Rohn said, "If two or three agree on a common purpose, then nothing is impossible." What's your common purpose that you are striving for? What does your future look like as you imagine it? Who do you want going with you?

The Five Characteristics of People You Need on Your Team

I know there are a lot of characteristics out there of value, but what I have found in people who have championed me personally and the athletes I have worked with over the years can be grouped into five characteristics.

I have one caveat and reminder for you as you think about the five characteristics of the people you want on your team. The expectation is that you also reflect the character you desire in others to show toward you. Others won't stick around long if they realize you want something from them that you are not willing to give back. So, this is a good opportunity to take another look at yourself as you look at those around you.

1. Selfless

It is no easy task to begin to imagine what the future may have in store and what possibly could be your next career. Having someone who is supportive of your decisions and willing to think about you and your interests first, not what they can get out of the decision, matters. Author Veronica Roth said, "It's when you're acting selflessly that you are at your bravest." The principle is the same in sport as well as in life. When you have your team's interests in mind first, rather than your own, you are focused on the team and the team's success. The power of your team is the willingness to help, build, and put the interests of each other above each individual.

One of the greatest examples of this is the pit crew in racing. They are solely judged, criticized, and analyzed on how fast they can finish their tasks and get the vehicle back out on the track. It is simply amazing what pit crews can accomplish; the speed, accuracy, focus, and knowing their roles. It is beauty in motion when you watch a trained, focused, and prepared pit crew go to work, but you may have to watch them in slow motion to see what they have done. Search "fastest Formula 1 pit stop," and you will see a video of Red

Bull racing with a pit stop of 1.82 seconds—it's amazing![9] Each individual knows their role and speed and ability to know the different responsibilities, and how the responsibilities fit together as a team. Let's follow the words of James Keller when he said, "A candle loses nothing by lighting another candle." Be *Selfless* today and light the candles of those around you and look to have others on your team that do the same!

2. Generous

So often when we think of the word generous, money is involved. Money is not the focus here. Generosity comes in many different forms and is given through many avenues. For generosity, let me clarify what I am talking about. Let's zero in on the personal resources others have to offer. For me, presence and time are the greatest assets someone can give. Winston Churchill understands this truth. "We make a living by what we get, but we make a life by what we give." You want others to be willing to give of their time and be present with you in the process, especially during those dark moments; that is when you most need others to lift you up.

Here is the reminder. You cannot expect of others what you yourself are not willing to give. As athletes, you are pulled in many directions—interviews, signings, and appearances, not to mention all of the responsibilities as a student-athlete with class, homework, and exams. But, if you desire to have others be generous with you and give of their resources, you also have to do the same. The Dalai Lama XIV said it well when he said, "Generosity is the most natural outward expression of an inner attitude of compassion and loving-kindness."

Seek out those who are generous with their actions, words, and time, and give the same. Remember, you are the sum total of the five people with whom you spend the most time. Choose wisely. Ancient Stoic, Seneca, implored that, "We should give as we would receive, cheerfully, quickly, and without hesitation; for there is no grace in a benefit that sticks to the fingers." Generosity is infectious and will spread and have significant impact on your life and those around you.

3. Loving

In sport, there are so many ups and downs—one day, you are man of the match, and the next, you are number one on the "not Top 10" on ESPN. A key characteristic for being a part of your team is that they care for and value you, not what you can provide for them or what they can get from you. No matter what decision you make, they will always love you and desire to be with you. You want others around you who value you and love you for yourself.

You are able to be yourself—not the you in front of the camera or the person you think you need to be when the fans are cheering, simply you. James A. Baldwin recognizes the power of taking off the mask and being yourself, and attributes love as the catalyst. "Love takes off masks that we fear we cannot live without and know we cannot live within." When you are around those who love you, you are fully known and are able to fully know others. Maya Angelou said, "Love recognizes no barriers. It jumps hurdles, leaps fences, penetrates walls to arrive at its destination full of hope." Love is the greatest and most powerful expression, action, and feeling we can experience in this life, and it is what spurs you on, whether in the dark moments of a valley or celebrations on the mountain top.

4. Patient

One thing I have realized after being around professional athletes for close to fifteen years is that athletes can be difficult to work with at times. Then again, so are people in general. There are personal preferences, likes, dislikes, hopes and dreams, visions of what should be, and the list goes on and on. The reality is that we are all different. We think differently, act differently, have different life experiences and personal preferences. Don't get me wrong; there are plenty of similarities, but like our fingerprints, we are all unique in our special way.

As an athlete, patience is key to find success in your sport and competition. Legendary basketball coach John Wooden said, "Before success comes patience. When we add to our accomplishments the element of hard work over a long period of time, we'll place a far greater value on the outcome. When we are patient, we'll have a greater appreciation of our success." So there is an importance to finding others who think the same way. There is an old adage that says, "Rome wasn't built in a day." It took time, and no matter how powerful Caesar was, he had to wait until it was built.

Thinking about what could be next for your life, let alone making a decision on what that could be, is a difficult task. Giving yourself the opportunity to be patient with the process and having others around you to encourage, speak into, and journey alongside you is key. Bruce Lee said, "Patience is not passive; on the contrary, it is concentrated strength." You don't want to be rushed, but encouraged, challenged, and pushed along the way as you go through the process of imagining the future and dreaming about what's next, even while you are still competing. Remember, it is better to be ready than early; the achievements that last take time, patience is essential!

5. People Smart

I was recently at a networking event, and I overheard someone say, 'be more interested than interesting.' It stopped me as I pondered the thought. Be more interested in the people you meet and interact with instead of focusing on being interesting to others. Dale Carnegie emphasized this point when he said, "You can make more friends in two months by becoming interested in other people than you can in two years by trying to get other people interested in you." Let's look at it this way. I am guessing here, but you have probably been around someone else who simply likes to hear themselves talk. No matter what you share, there is an attempt to one-up your story or what was said, or they completely ignore what you shared and only talk about something related to themselves. It's obnoxious and a put-off to others!

There is power and opportunity in the ability for people to read someone else's tone of voice, body language, and facial expressions. Understanding expressions and body language is significant in communicating and understanding what is being said. I jumped over to Google U and searched for "how much communication is nonverbal." One of the first things to come up was the 7-38-55 Rule. The main premise of the rule is that 7 percent of what is communicated is through the words we use, 38 percent is the tone that is used when words are spoken, and 55 percent is the individual's body language.[10] I know there are exceptions to the rule, but those numbers speak volumes. It is important that you have people around you, as well as yourself, who need to have and develop the skill to read other people's body language and tone of voice, not only hear the words coming out of their mouths.

The thought of beginning to dream and think about something other than your sport could feel crazy and daunting, and if we are being honest, not really that important. But what is important is having the right people around you to champion, encourage, and build into you as you go through this process. You want someone to hear what you are saying and understand who you are as you navigate this difficult process and who you want on your team moving forward. Patrick Lencioni, in his book *The Ideal Team Player,* boils it down when he says, "*They* ask good questions, listen to what others are saying, and stay engaged in conversation intently... *they* have good judgement and intuition around the subtleties of group dynamics and the impact of their words and actions."[11] Your team members need to be people-smart and be willing to interact and invest in you and those on your team well!

Go Farther *Together*

When you look to the future, it can seem daunting, ambiguous, big, and distant; the idea or thought of going after it all by yourself seems hopeless or a waste of time. There is joy when you can share experiences and moments with others. When you begin to dream and think about what could be, bring a few key people along with you. Get their perspective, dream together, and go after what could be as a team—you'll go far!

Having the confidence in understanding yourself, your story, identity, and values helps you know who works well with you, who you will work best with, and who will get the best out of you as you navigate inter-relational conflict, differences, ideas, and dreams. This is your life, your dreams, and your future beyond your sport. You want people to go after what's best for you from your perspective, not their hopes and dreams.

You know what you know. You want to be pushed to think and challenged but not overwhelmed. These five characteristics are essential for those in your corner. One quick side note is that there may be people you want in your corner or by your side that don't have these characteristics. The good news is that all five characteristics can be developed and cultivated. So you have your team, but you need to work on developing these character skills with them.

It is important to have the right people around you. Identify who will champion you without strings attached, that one person who will be in your corner whether you fail or not and who isn't with you to get something from you. Trust is key and essential; who do you trust to get you to where you want to go? You can create/establish your team, a group of three to five people who will look out for you and what you want to go after. Now is the time to *Imagine the Future* and go together!

PART 4
FOCUS

Always remember,
your focus determines your reality.

—George Lucas

Recently, my daughter was playing with her microscope set. Microscopes are fun tools to use. You get an object or liquid, and you put it on a glass window, shine light at it, and then through a magnifying lens to see what it's made of by taking a closer look at the object or liquid. Well, she had gathered a few things from outside, mainly leaves from a few different trees, that she wanted to take a closer, more in-depth look at—the colors, veins, and different aspects of each.

She set the microscope up on the table, got a light to reflect from the mirror through the glass, set the magnification she wanted, and then looked through the scope with excitement!

Nothing! Well, almost nothing. All she saw was fuzziness and blurriness with a green tint.

She checked again to make sure she had all of the pieces in place, but again, all she got was a green fuzzy and blurry something. She called me to look, so I join her. I looked at the scope, the setup, and the light source to make sure everything was in order. Then I peered through the scope and realized what was going on. She had set up the microscope the correct way, set the magnification, and the leaf was placed properly. She merely needed to dial in the scope so that the object would be brought into focus. A few turns on the dial, and there it was, a clear picture of the leaf, its veins, and vibrant green color.

She had everything she needed to see the object. She had done the work of gathering the objects from outside, set up her microscope, put everything together to view it, and even got an additional light source in case the natural light wasn't bright enough. When it came to viewing the object, it still wasn't clear, and she needed to bring it all into focus.

In the fourth step in the SHIFT framework, you will intentionally take the time to *Focus* and bring clarity as you move forward. You have worked hard to gather information and understanding about yourself, your identity, values, and passion, and you have even dreamed about the future. Now, you are taking all of what you have gathered and prepared and bringing it into *Focus*, making what you have discovered and where you desire to go clear. *Focus* leads to clarity, much like turning the dial on the microscope brought clarity. Clarity doesn't happen by accident; action is needed to gain focus and taking the time to invest in yourself as you move forward toward clarity in life beyond your sport. Let's go and get focused!

CHAPTER 10

THINKING WITH THE END IN MIND REVISITED

If you don't take the time to focus on what
matters, then you're living a life of someone
else's design.

—Tony Robbins

I loved the maze games when I was growing up! Whether it was a book of mazes you bought at the store or the kid's menu at a local restaurant, I enjoyed the game and needed to solve the problem. Not sure if it was a ploy by my parents to keep me occupied while at a restaurant, long car rides as a family, or simply a problem to solve, it was fun for me. It was a way to pass the time, and yes, this was pre-iPhone and tablet days. Anyway, I am not sure why or who I learned this from, but there was a little trick I would do to solve the maze faster. I would always start at the finish of the maze and work my way back to the start. For whatever reason, it seemed logical and easier for me to begin at the end rather than work harder from the beginning. I'm not sure if it was an efficiency thing or speed, but the reality was the same; it was always easier to start at the end of the maze. What I realized was that the closer you got to the finish, the number of options and turns available to you decreased.

This same idea and perspective are also true for sport. Think about your last season. When you began the season, the goal for yourself and your team was to win the championship. You may have had other goals in place, like conference championships, supporters shield, or some statistical numbers, but ultimately, you wanted to win the championship.

With that goal at the forefront, you visualize yourself holding the trophy and then work your way back to your current reality in pre-season. Then you map out your very own *GPS* for the season by planning accordingly to achieve your desired result—the championship. By focusing on the end goal and starting there, you are able to eliminate many of the distractions and options, and you don't get bogged down or waste time going down other dead ends. Sure, you will have a few detours along the way, but the desired outcome of winning the championship remains the same. Similarly, when you accidentally take a wrong turn or miss your turn, your *GPS* reroutes you to get back on track.

There is a similar perspective for life, leadership, and goal setting that author and leadership expert, Stephen Covey, made famous. In Covey's book *The 7 Habits of Highly Effective People,* one of the habits is, "Start with the end in mind." The first principle in *Focus* is "Start with the end in Mind" revisited. In this chapter, I want you to begin to zero in on the process of getting to your destination. When you start with the end in mind, your next step or progression is to work back to where you are, the present. Now, you can't account for everything that will take place along the journey, but you can learn, grow, and develop along the way. While you keep the destination in mind, you also focus on the present and the process.

Develop as You Go

Today, most people don't go for a ride or go cruising in their vehicle. Years ago, there was this thing that people would do called going on *Sunday drives*. An individual or even the entire family would get into the car and drive without a specific destination. The only goal was to enjoy the scenery, time together, and exploring new territory they had never seen before. That may sound different or foreign, but there is something to the premise and idea of Sunday drives.

Today, when you get into your vehicle of choice, there is a destination in mind. You are going somewhere you have already been, so you start driving toward your destination, or you put the address or location into your phone and follow the GPS.

The focus is all on the destination. When you think with the end in mind, the destination is identified, but the road or process to get there isn't fixed. Thinking with the end in mind, you still have the joy of the journey, similar to those Sunday drives, where you enjoy the moment while taking in all that's around you.

What I would like to revisit, with the idea of thinking with the end in mind, is that it's not a destination like a geographic location or championship podium, but rather a process of growth and development. From my experience, coaches and players, when talking about this principle of thinking with the end in mind, are referring to the end of the season and winning the conference, winning the championship, or being first in the division, etc. The irony is that when you dive into Covey's content, he emphasizes the importance of imagination, the mental aspect of fortitude and strength, and envisioning what your best true self could look like while you journey. In the training overview of "Thinking With the End in Mind," Covey states,

> *Habit 2 is based on imagination--the ability to envision in your mind what you cannot at present see with your eyes. It is based on the principle that all things are created twice. There is a mental (first) creation, and a physical (second) creation. The physical creation follows the mental, as a building follows a blueprint. If you don't make a conscious effort to visualize who you are and what you want in life, then you empower other people and circumstances to shape you and your life by default. It's about connecting again with your own uniqueness and then defining the personal, moral, and ethical guidelines within which you can most happily express and fulfill yourself.[12]*

Thinking with the end in mind revisited isn't a vocation, position, championship, or even a specific financial goal. Thinking with the end in mind is the idea of who you desire to become based on your imagination first and then realized and actualized through your actions and choices, the process. The building is created from the specs of the blueprint, not the other way around. If you are living at your best, what does that look like? How would you be expressed and experienced by others when at your best? It is not about specific results per se but focused on who you are becoming and what your best looks like reflected through your actions, lifestyle, mindset, and character. It's about truly reflecting and examining what you are capable of accomplishing today and coupling that with your capacity of tomorrow.

Destination Redefined

I won't go into much detail here about the process of choosing a destination since we already covered this topic in a previous chapter, but I want to share a few highlights and create a change in your perspective about your destination. If the end in mind is an idea of who you desire to become, let's think of the end as when you leave this physical Earth. If your death is the end, and you don't know exactly when that will occur, what will it look like today for you to be at your best emotionally, physically, intellectually, spiritually, and relationally? Thinking with the end in mind allows you to eliminate multiple dead ends, like starting at the finish line of the maze, and allows you to minimize choices, thoughts, attitudes, behaviors, mindset, limiting beliefs, and self-talk. By revisiting *starting with the end in mind*, you are creating a filter through which you view life, sport, relationships, and the world around you.

Let me introduce you to author and artist Charlie Mackesy. He wrote about redefining one's perspective about life, relationships, and how we view the world in his book *The Boy, the Mole, the Fox and the Horse*. Mackesy writes with whimsy, coupled with beautiful art and illustration. The story begins with a boy talking to a mole, and the dialogue helps us redefine our destination and the process. The mole asks the boy, "What do you want to be when you grow up?" "Kind," said the boy. "What do you think success is?" asked the boy. "To love," said the mole.

What I am curious about is how would you have answered those same questions. When you were younger, was it your dream to be a professional athlete, successful businesswoman, or even own a business? How about success? Did you define it as winning trophies, championships, large contract, power, fame, or having your name all over social media? When you look at your life, one of the hardest aspects is seeing beyond the moment in front of you and the single-minded focus of winning and athletic success, but there is so much more to this life and the impact you can have within it.

The reality is that we don't know exactly when we will leave this Earth, but it will happen at some point. Our lives are finite whether we acknowledge it or not. So, what does it look like for you to make the most of your life, your time here on Earth? You are more than the game you play. Your performance isn't what defines you or what determines your significance and value. You have so much to offer this world and specifically the people you interact with each day. My hope is that you maximize your life and impact to the fullest, which does include, but isn't limited to, athletic success. To do that, the long term and redefined perspective of thinking with the end in mind has to be clear.

3D Obstacles

What I have discovered is that while this process isn't complicated, it also isn't easy. Thinking with the end in mind revisited comes with the realities of life, and in life, there is so much over which you have zero control. Ten percent of life is what happens to you, but 90 percent of your life is how you respond to your reality.[13] Again, there is very little that is actually within your control, but how you navigate life and your circumstances will determine the impact you have in the lives of others and how far you go. I have identified the **3D Obstacles** that athletes experience in sport and life, and I am here to help guide you through them. These obstacles come from anywhere and at any time, so be prepared as you explore, redefine, and revisit your reality!

1. Power of Distractions: Limit them, or they will limit you.

Distractions are all around us, whether it be dings, buzzes, text messages, ads, pop-ups, emails, interruptions, shiny things, or vibrations from our phones. That is only scratching the surface of the distractions in our world today. Have you ever gone through an entire day and thought to yourself, "What did I actually do today?" I have, and as I reflect on the day, there is one distraction after another, one fire to put out after another, things that seemed urgent in the moment yet really added no value or helped move the development or growth *needle* forward. Winston Churchill said, "You will never reach your destination if you stop and throw rocks at every dog that barks." In our world today, the dogs are barking loud and often.

Have you ever watched a parade with horses? In Delaware, OH, where my wife Rachel grew up, each fall during the Delaware County Fair, the country hosts the All Horse Parade. It is amazing to see the various horses, riders, and of course, the *pooper scoopers* dressed funnily as they walk behind the horses cleaning up the messes. What's interesting is that a number of the horses have these guards next to their eyes that limit where and what they can see. It creates a tunnel vision of sorts so that the horses can only see and focus on what's in front of them and limits the number of distractions around them so they can walk the streets calmly while hundreds of people cheer and watch them on either side.

Thinking with the end in mind revisited helps you create your own figurative tunnel vision. It limits the distractions all around and helps you focus on what's most important. You will be distracted at some point—we all are—but by having a clear idea of what the end will look like helps you create a healthy tunnel vision to prevent distractions from limiting your impact in your sport and throughout your life. Take to heart the words of Stephen Covey when he said, "Your most important work is always ahead of you, never behind you." I truly believe this for you and your life. You may not see it this way, especially when you begin to think about the reality that someday you will not be playing and competing in your sport. Perhaps you still talk about the glory days of competing, but it is true; your athletic career will eventually go, and the best is yet to come. Your greatest work and impact is ahead of you, so don't get distracted by the barking dogs!

2.   Beware of Disorientation: Patience breeds clarity.

Concussions are no joke! For those who have experienced them, they are difficult to navigate, and at a young age, you don't fully realize the gravity or long-term impact they can have on your mind, brain, and body. I still remember the first concussion I got playing soccer. I was 19 and competing in the Professional Development League with a team from Michigan. A forward on the opposing team blindsided me with an elbow to the head, and to be honest, I don't remember much after that. What I could piece together was being helped off the field and then being at home. The seriousness and issue from not remembering much from that game was that I lived in Michigan, but the game was played in Indiana. I don't remember the rest of the game or even how I got back home to Michigan. It is scary to look back at that moment and have no memory to go along with it.

> I will never forget that feeling of helplessness and disorientation. I was there, but I wasn't present; my body was awake, but I wasn't feeling like myself.

After a number of weeks, I was cleared to go back to competing, but I will never forget that feeling of helplessness and disorientation. I was there, but I wasn't present; my body was awake, but I wasn't feeling like myself. Sometimes life, sport, relationships, and experiences hit us the same way. They create a disorientation effect in our minds and our present reality.

To bring this point a bit closer, I was recently talking with a professional athlete about his recovery from injury. He had a significant injury that sidelined him for a number of months. He shared about the confusion and the fogginess of his present state emotionally and psychologically. He was at the training facility but separated from the team. He was present but not connected; he was there but felt absent and isolated. He was disoriented with his current reality, progression, and space. He said he was going through days as if they were nothing, not remembering what he was doing or why. So, I started asking questions about the season, his role with the team, what he desired to accomplish individually and collectively with the team. I am not a sport psychologist or counselor; I merely asked questions to help him clarify the destination and direction he desired to go. As he continued to rehab over the coming weeks, his perspective shifted, and his intensity and focus increased. He was able to see more clearly; the fog lifted, and he had a visible picture of where he was going. Thinking with the end in mind revisited and having that clear picture gives clarity and patience in those moments when the fog rolls in and your next step isn't fully visible. Thinking with the end mind revisited releases the power that disorientation can have in your life and gives you clarity to continue moving forward.

3.   Disasters Happen: How will you respond?

How do you plan for a global pandemic? I don't know either. Regardless of your opinions on how things were managed, handled, and led in the US and around the world, the scope and impact of the COVID-19 virus were obvious and felt by all throughout the world. How did you respond? As an athlete, what was your perspective and plan as seasons were cancelled, postponed, delayed, and rescheduled? I have experienced strikes, walk-outs, and other delays to sporting events, but never the cancellation of entire seasons, postponement until further notice, or competition bubbles. New territory for all involved!

As the pandemic continued with postponements of seasons in the spring of 2020, I received a call from a professional soccer player I was coaching. When he called, the pro soccer season in the US had been postponed, and in most states, businesses were shut down, and people were being required to quarantine and isolate from others. He said, "I know I am wasting my time, but I don't know what to do. I wake up, work out, and then do basically nothing the rest of the day. I am wasting my time, but I don't know what to do or even what the next step looks like. Can you help?"

Can you relate? What was your experience during COVID-19 as an athlete being separated from your team and coaching staff? What were you doing with all of your additional time, your days not completely scheduled by other people or the team or club? Could you resonate with this athlete and what he was experiencing?

There isn't a clear-cut guide on how to navigate a global pandemic successfully as an athlete, or for a businessperson, teacher, construction worker, parent, adult, or kid. So, how do you navigate an environment and circumstance that is completely out of your control yet requires you to navigate by yourself or even possibly lead others through it? In the journey of life and sport, rarely do you have a straight line; there are turns, ups, downs, reverses, and a myriad of other movements required, but what keeps you going, moving forward in the midst of the unknown? Disasters happen, but when you have the end in mind revisited, you are able to readjust your path, make changes, reroute, and keep going. How you respond is what will make a lasting impact on yourself and those around you. Your attitude, actions, and perspective are key, and thinking with the end in mind revisited will guide your steps in the midst of those unknown and unexpected moments.

Stay Focused

Martin Luther King Jr. had a dream that one day all men would be treated equal. He eloquently gave his famous "I Have a Dream" speech with a hope and vision of the truth that all men and women are created and treated equal. In the midst of civil unrest, struggles, and backlash, he continued forward, challenging people to continue on. "If you can't fly, run; if you can't run, walk; if you can't walk, crawl, but by all means keep moving." Distractions, Disorientations, and Disasters come around subtlety and sometimes violently, but these 3D obstacles are real. They are part of our lives and will hit us like a ton of bricks, unexpectedly and having a serious effect on our lives. As you navigate the present, knowing where you are going gives focus, clarity, purpose, and drive to keep moving. So, as you prepare today, think with the end in mind revisited!

Let me finish this chapter with a challenge from Bruce Lee. "The successful warrior is the average man with laser-like focus." Stay focused on the journey as you move closer and closer each day to the end. Make the most of your days, and don't allow Distractions, Disorientations, or Disasters limit the purpose and impact you have been created for here on Earth!

CHAPTER 11
CLARIFY WHAT SUCCESS MEANS TO YOU

Try not to become a man of success.
Rather become a man of value.

—Albert Einstein

How will you know if you are a winner? I remember thinking about this early in life. For me, a winner was whoever had the most points at the end of the game or could jump the highest on the playground or finished the race before anyone else. It also meant being the one who finished the puzzle by putting in the last piece and the member of my family who could eat their food the fastest. Being a winner meant being number one in your own eyes and in the eyes of those around you. Success equaled being a winner, and being a winner was success. But is being a winner the measure of what actually is success or being successful? Is success a metric you can quantify and answer yes or no to once the dust settles around you? The irony of success is that to determine whether or not something or someone is successful can be subjective to those involved. Success can come in different shapes and sizes.

In sport, success is most often measured through winning, which means you accumulated more points than anyone else or the other team. Complete the race or course before anyone else. Success is occupying the top stand on the podium, topping the leader board, and being number one.

Think about this perspective: One man's success can be another man's failure. Do you agree with that? Does it resonate with you, or does that idea repulse you? As an athlete, failure is a regular occurrence in training and competition. It is those moments of failure that make you and other athletes great. Michael Jordan highlighted that reality when he said, "The key to success is failure. I've missed more than 9,000 shots in my career. I've lost almost 300 games. Twenty-six times I've been trusted to take the game-winning shot and missed. I've failed over and over and over again in my life. And that is why I succeed." Pushing boundaries, pushing our bodies, pushing our mental capacities, and striving toward greatness is riddled with failure. But are results the only indicator of success and being a winner?

Defining Success

There have been some talented and amazing athletes at the pro level who have never won a championship. Would they be categorized as unsuccessful or not winners? Growing up in Michigan, the road to success is a troubled one when it comes to the Detroit Lions. The

Lions are one of four teams never to play in a Super Bowl, and disappointment is usually what you experience as a fan, rather than any form of success or winning. For ten amazing years when I was growing up, there was Barry Sanders. Sanders is still arguably one of the most dynamic, elusive, and explosive running backs of all time in the NFL.

More often than not, I would watch the Lions to see what he would do next. Sanders could take a broken play, run more yards side to side and behind the line of scrimmage, and then all of a sudden break tackles and end up in the end zone. He had the ability to stop and move on a dime, and even one time faked Hall of Fame cornerback, Rod Woodson, so badly that it ended his season due to a knee ligament injury. Watching Barry Sanders was mesmerizing!

I loved watching Barry Sanders play and compete. I still remember holding my Barry Sanders TOPS football card, wishing and hoping that he would win the rushing title that 1990 season. We already knew they wouldn't win the Super Bowl, but I hoped at least we could win something that season. During the final game of the season, Sanders needed 168 yards to win the title, and he ended the game with 158 yards. It was heartbreaking for me, but there is more to the story.

The head coach, Wayne Fontes, was notified on the sidelines with over a minute left to go in the game about Sanders being only ten yards short of winning the rushing title, and the Lions had the ball. He asked Barry about going back in, gaining those 10 yards, and winning the rushing title. Sanders said, "Let's just win and go home."[14] At a later time, he was asked why, and he replied, "When everyone is out for statistics—you know, individual fulfillment—that's when trouble starts. I don't want to ever fall victim to that."[15] Christian

Okoye of the Kansas City Chiefs went on to win the rushing title that year, but for Sanders and the Lions, they won the game and went home.

When I look at Barry Sanders and his career, he accomplished some amazing things as a running back, but neither playing in nor winning the Super Bowl was one of them. He has accomplished individual records, rushing over 2000 yards in a season, Pro Bowls, and All-League accolades, but he never won the championship. So, was he successful? I can't speak for him, but when I think about Barry Sanders and the joy watching him brought to my life, the answer is *yes*.

According to him, he was ready to retire and be done. He even told a few teammates he was done after the last game of the 1998 season in Baltimore. Even though Sanders had signed a multi-year contract only the year before, he opted instead to walk away from the game. If numbers remained consistent for that next season, he would have passed Walter Payton as the NFL's all-time leading rusher. Yet, the accolades, frustrations, and physical and emotional toll was enough. Sanders shared, "I had already achieved a level of success that gave me much satisfaction and pride. I didn't need to pass Walter to prove that to myself."[16]

Barry Sanders, who is still the fourth-leading NFL rusher of all time with 15,269 yards, left the game after he decided what success in the game looked like for him. Many, including me, doubted his decision to walk away from the game and retire. It broke my heart. But success and life looked different for Sanders and his perspective on what success is. Success can be defined in multiple ways, and the way you want success to be defined is imperative and needs to be clarified. How you define success is a guardrail for your life and keeps you focused as you navigate through your sport, as an athlete, and life after sport.

Look for Growth Opportunities

Early in my career with Athletes in Action, I was working with and mentoring athletes at Ohio State University. One day, I was at the football training facility with a handful of other AIA staff, and the then-head football coach Jim Tressel came by to say hello. We were talking about competition, winning, and the work it takes to be successful year after year. While we were talking, Coach Tressel asked, "How do you know if you are a winner?" I was thinking about wins, loses, championships, etc., and that is what we talked about. Then Coach Tressel asked more poignantly, "How do you know if you are a winner at life?"

That was one of the earliest moments I can remember thinking about my life in the context of winning and thinking about success beyond sport and competition. That may have been one of the first times I considered that perhaps success in sport, in the way I had historically thought of success, wins and championships, wasn't what I should be using to define success for life or sport. What does it mean to be a winner in the locker room with my teammates, in the community, and now for me as a father, husband, friend, citizen in our community? That day I began to reframe how I thought about and viewed success, and I want to challenge you to start doing the same.

In the context of sport, whether you win or lose, great players and teams can pull out positives from the competition. You can learn from the game and improve and get better. That is how even when you lose, you can also win.

Carol Dweck, in her book *Mindset*, emphasizes this point when describing legendary UCLA basketball coach, John Wooden, and his growth mindset about success.

He didn't ask for mistake-free games. He didn't demand that his players never lose. He asked for full preparation and full effort from them. "Did I win? Did I lose? Those are the wrong questions. The correct question is: Did I make my best effort?" If so, he says, "You may be outscored but you will never lose."[17]

Emphasizing this point later in Wooden's life and philosophy, Coach Wooden shared at a TED X event in 2001 what success and winning meant to him and how he defined it. Wooden's definition of success is "peace of mind attained only through self-satisfaction and knowing you made the effort you did the best you are capable."[18] As an elite athlete, you want to win, but success, for Wooden, is not only about the results, records, or winning and losing. It is also about your character, your capacity, ability to adapt, and seeing every circumstance as a growth opportunity.

How Much Is Enough?

You have to be competitive and have a desire to win, but being successful doesn't mean you don't fail, and it doesn't mean failure and losses are negatives. Failing and making mistakes are opportunities to get better, improve, and progress, and that same growth mindset can be applied as you prepare for life after sport.

The allure and the strong pull of sport culture drive home the idea of what is success, and the definition of success usually falls within the areas of money and/ or possessions (net financial worth), power (position, influence, role, history), and love (sex, beauty of significant other or partner, soulmate). The harsh reality, though, is, how much is enough? How much money do you need to have until you believe you have been successful? How much power and influence? Do you have to find the perfect partner or have sex a certain number of times and with a certain number of people to be considered successful?

There is an unknown when you follow along with the popular definitions of success. These three areas may be what success looks like to you. But what does? Does your definition of success align with who you are, your identity, your values, and where you want to go? When targets are subjective, they are elusive, and it is like trying to catch smoke in your hands. You will be asking yourself, "How much is enough?" You need to clarify what success is for you!

Eleven Clarifying Questions

There is an old saying, "One man's trash is another man's treasure." This same adage can be applied to defining success. One athlete can be completely fixed on winning the game and the result, and whenever they lose, it's viewed as a failure and not a winner. Another athlete can look at any situation or result and find something positive (a success) within it. Learn from the experience, grow, and improve; therefore, declaring the experience and circumstance successful. Booker T. Washington said, "Success is to be measured not so much by the position that one has reached in life as by the obstacles which he has overcome while trying to succeed." When you know how you define success, you begin to see it in multiple areas of your life. Even the simplest of successes are moments to celebrate. When you know what success is for you, the obstacles that occur in your life become opportunities to overcome and grow. When you clarify success, you will begin to see those obstacles as opportunities for development and growth through a positive filter. When you overcome those obstacles, you believe and know you have experienced success.

Clarifying what success means for you creates a clear definition to filter through the ups and downs of sport, your athletic career, and life as a whole. You may make some decisions that don't work out, you may choose a destination you end up not liking at all, and you may run into a few dead ends, but that's okay. You have the opportunity to refocus, think about a new direction, and keep moving forward toward success.

Clarifying what success means for you creates a clear definition to filter through the ups and downs of sport, your athletic career, and life as a whole.

So, let's get practical for a moment here. You may be asking, "How do you actually define success for yourself?" Coach Wooden didn't like the current definition in the dictionary for success, so he came up with his own. Why not do the same? Don't chase society's definition of success or someone else's; come up with your own. You don't want to miss those moments of success along the way in sport or in life because you are chasing something someone else defined for you. Envision what success means for you, and remember, successful development starts with the blueprint, then the building. Take time to create your success blueprint. You must visualize success before you achieve it! How will you define success for you and your life? How will you know you are a winner?

Here are eleven questions to help and guide you along in the process of defining what success is for you.[19]

1. How do you want to be remembered as an athlete, and what is your athletic legacy?
2. What do you want to be shared and talked about once you are done competing?
3. How does your athletic legacy align with the legacy you desire to leave for your entire life?
4. How will you know you are aligned with your athletic and life legacy?
5. What are your life themes and common threads in your life that you would use to define yourself?
6. What have you done that aligns with your why, passion, and values?
7. What do you view as impact work or actions that could change the world of others?
8. If you could fast forward twelve months from now, how would you know you have been successful?
9. What will winning look like for you after you are done competing? At the end of your life?
10. Whose athletic career and life do you admire and why?
11. What five words would you use to define success for yourself?

After answering these eleven questions, look for commonalities or similarities between the answers as you begin to write out your definition. What makes you unique and successful is you, what you bring to the table, your unique skill-set, personality, values, abilities, and mindset. Don't fall for the trap that you must define success the same as how the sport culture has defined it: money, power, and love. Work to put together a sentence or two that describes what success is for you.

Your definition may include some or part of cultures definitions, and that's okay. Be clear on what success is for you and how you will continue to move forward toward that success. There isn't a one-size-fits-all definition, and success can be defined in many ways. When you are at your best, continue down that path, and discover the successes that are in front of you. The beauty of life and sport are the choices you get to make as you journey through it. Clarify what success is for you, so at the end of your life, you know you have been a *winner*!

CHAPTER 12

FINDING BALANCE:
THE POWER OF SAYING *NO* AND *YES*

Focus is about saying no.

—Steve Jobs

I remember the first time I saw a Power Balance bracelet. A baseball player on ESPN had this new, cool bracelet with a hologram embedded in it. By wearing it, the holographic technology would tap into and align with the natural energy field in your body and around you and help stabilize and give you added balance. I wanted to get one so badly! It seemed like every athlete I knew was wearing one, from the NBA to the MLB, to university athletes, and even celebrities and politicians. If these elite athletes were wearing them, I needed to wear it as well!

Maintaining balance is key as an athlete, especially when the sport and action are moving so quickly. You get wrong-footed or leaning in the opposite direction, and your opponent is able to get past you. Whether a cross-over in basketball or juke, a shoulder fake from a running back, the ability to maintain an edge in skiing, or powerlifting in the Olympics, balance is essential for success.

The irony of these Power Balance hologram bracelets was that it was a sham, a fake. Olympic Gymnastic Dominque Dawes, along with sixteen other volunteers, participated in a test put on by members of an Independent Investigations Group of the bracelet and its effect on athletes.[20] The study had half of the athletes wear the bracelet and the other half a placebo bracelet. Then the two groups switched. The results were basically the same for both groups, whether they were wearing the bracelet or the placebo bracelet.

In addition, Mark Cuban, owner of the Dallas Mavericks, was quoted in an article on ESPN saying, "See this stuff?" as he grabbed the display of Power Balance bracelets. "It was a scam when they were on 'Shark Tank.' It's still a scam. I don't care if the NBA was dumb enough to sign an agreement; this is going where it belongs."[21] Cuban then took the display and threw it into the trash. People and athletes will go to crazy lengths to gain an edge, even use props or gimmicks at even the thought of giving an advantage or level up in sport and life.

Weighing In

Have you ever fallen into the trap of only looking to gain an edge in your sport, only to realize there are other aspects of your life that are out of balance or off-kilter? Finding rhythm or balance athletically is important, as it keeps you grounded and stable. The same reality is true for you in your life. In ancient times, vendors would use a scale to determine the value of something sold in the market, whether it was grain, wheat, barley, oil, or even precious metals. They all have value based on their weight. So, merchants who were unethical would travel with a balance and two sets of weights. They would have one set that would represent the correct specific weight for each item sold so the buyer could see what it weighed and know its price, but they would also travel with a second set of weights that leaned in their favor. The fake weights would have the same appearance and likeness as the correct weights. They would weigh less; that way, the person making the purchase would have to pay more for less of whatever you were buying. Solomon, one of the wisest men of all time, said in his book of Proverbs four different times as a warning that unequal weights are an abomination to God, but just weights are a delight. Abomination is a strong word, and the dictionary defines it as "a thing that causes disgust or hatred."[22] Solomon was emphasizing the importance of acting, doing business, and competing in an honorable and true manner.

When looking at your life, balance is key. If you are competing, living, recovering, and eating all focused on your sport, you are not balanced, and things can go wrong, and damage can be done at various levels. You may not experience the negative effects right away, but the lifestyle and behavior eventually catch up with you. There is truth in the ancient proverb about equal balances and being cautious about having balance in your life as an athlete. The struggle is that you are singularly focused on your sport. So, where and how does balance fit into your life and competition?

Saying Yes to No

Let me introduce an idea to you. You have the power to choose, and understanding the power you have when you say no is vital for your success as an athlete and in life. When you have clarity on where you are going and the goals in place to get there, the ability to say *no* is as powerful as your *yes* and creates balance in your life. I would even go as far as making the statement that your *no* is more powerful. One of the greatest financial investors of our era, Warren Buffett, emphasized the importance of balance. "Knowing what to leave out is just as important as knowing what to focus on." You will need to know what, who, and why you say *no* and say *yes* to be clear and focus on what's most important and necessary to move forward. Buffett emphasized the importance of not only knowing what to leave out, what to say *no* to but also what to focus on and when to say *yes*.

> "Knowing what to leave out is just as important as knowing what to focus on."
> —Warren Buffett

Focusing in and being your own gatekeeper is important to move forward as an athlete and as you move into life after sport. Being an athlete is so much more than going to the gym, putting on your shoes, and shooting baskets. To reach the elite level, the depth of commitment, sacrifice, tenacity, grit, and focus needed is off the charts. Now, thinking through Name, Image, and Likeness while competing in the NCAA and developing a personal brand is going to take more investment from you. You will need to discover and decide what it will look like to manage your brand, learning how to market yourself, preparing for life after sport, or navigating the transition in your post-competing phase. Knowing what to leave out and what to focus on creates confidence, clarity, and balance throughout your life.

As an athlete, even at an early age, you have had people around you asking for something: tickets, jerseys, autographs, selfies, endorsements. When the crowds, media, clubs, friends and family are surrounding you asking for a thousand different things and the distractions are numerous, have you ever stopped to think about all of the things you are doing and what you actually want? How do you desire to display yourself, what causes, ideas, or people do you want to align yourself to for branding and marketing? How do you want to be remembered as an athlete and as a human? When I consult with pro athletes, one of the most common regrets I hear is that the athlete did not start preparing for life after sport sooner. I get it; it is hard when you are twenty, twenty-one, or twenty-two and trying to think or have clarity about what you want to be associated with or brand-affiliated. One key to finding balance and a healthy rhythm is knowing what to say *no* to so you are able to say *yes* to what's right and best for you.

The Power of No

How do you make decisions moving forward, and what is the focus you desire to create the greatest possible space for you to be successful? In the previous chapter, we talked about the importance of defining what success is for you. Business owner and author, Missy Yost, wrote about nineteen various definitions of success; Number eight was about the power of your no. Yost states, "Success only comes with a balanced life. Part of balance is learning to say no. Saying no doesn't mean you are selfish; it simply means you have priorities and know what you need to give your attention to at any given time."[23]

Did you catch that?

For you to have successful balance in your life, you have to say *no*, and that is not selfish. What saying *no* means is that you have clarity, know your priorities, and what's most important to you and for you—not your agent, your friends, the media, coaches, or even family. Saying *no* also means you know what you need to focus in on and gives you time, your most valuable asset, as you pursue success in your sport, vocation, and life.

Your ability to say *no* is one of the greatest strengths you can develop, and to encourage you a bit, the reality is, you already are pretty good at it. Think back to all the times you have sacrificed for your sport. Every time you were saying *yes* to your sport—training, recovery, film, weight training—you were saying *no* to something else. You had a goal, vision, and a destination in mind, so you worked hard to create a path to achieve it. By doing so, you intentionally said *no* to opportunities along the way, even good opportunities, but they were not the best. Competing at the highest level was what you were pursuing. The dream of competing professionally created a clear path for you to navigate, and anything that limited or hindered you, you stiff-armed it and kept running!

Finding Focus with No

I'm not sure about you, but it wasn't always easy for me to say *no* to some things. Wanting to go out with friends, social activities, travel, eating certain foods, getting good sleep and intentional recovery; all those are things I said *no* to so I could be able to say *yes* to my sport and be successful.

If you think about it, you were actually practicing part of the *SHIFT* framework and didn't know it. You were passionate and motivated with a *why*, you had a clear destination, you had a vision for what success looked like, and you had an end in mind. By focusing on the journey ahead, you made the conscious decision to say *no* to something that would pave the way toward what you wanted to achieve, namely athletic success.

So how do you train yourself to learn how and know what and when to say *no* or *yes*?

Balance is the key! The ability to be balanced physically is of the utmost importance as you compete in sport and life, and balance will guide you toward success as you navigate transitions in sport, competition, and life. Here are three keys to adapt into your life that will need to be developed and cultivated as you create and achieve the results you desire. These keys are a result of finding balance through the power of the *no's* you choose, and they will help guide and give you confidence as you move forward.

Keys to Finding Balance by Reinforcing the Power of Your *No*

Saying *no* to something or someone means you are saying *yes* to something or someone else.

Sir Isaac Newton came to that realization when he wrote the third law of motion that states for every action, there is an equal and opposite reaction. What that means is that for each interaction, you make the choice to say *yes* or *no*; there is an equal action going in the opposite direction. So, when you say *yes* to training ten minutes longer, you are delaying by ten minutes whatever it was you had planned after the training. If you say *no* to going out late with friends, you are saying *yes* to getting more sleep and recovery.

In the *Focus* step, you are building off the foundation you built as you navigated through the first three steps. There is intentionality to having clarity and knowing who you are, your story, your values, your life themes, and the importance of your experience. In addition, by imagining the future, you are thinking and dreaming about your life after playing professionally. Moreover, your confidence continues to increase in knowing when and where to say *no* so you can say *yes* to what's most important.

For every *no*, there is an equal and opposite *yes* you are agreeing to pursue. Athletically, you have practiced this time and time again. You have sacrificed to get where you are today athletically, and you have cultivated the fortitude and strength on when to use your power of no. There is a natural cause and effect for the decisions you make each day, and knowing this reality for your sport and in life helps you maintain balance in both. How do you know when to choose no or yes? That brings us to the next key realizations necessary to understand and leverage the power of your no.

Commitment is needed to know when and why you say yes and no.

A *no* at the right time is as important and influential as your *yes*. When you are committed and know what you want and where you are going, commitment is the key to focus in on what's most important. Commitment is the vehicle that gives you the confidence to say *no* to a good opportunity to say *yes* to a great opportunity.

I remember the first time I drove through Atlanta. As a twelve year old, I was amazed looking out the window and counting eight lanes on either side. It was crazy for me coming from Michigan, where most roads only had two lanes. Even though there were a ton of lanes to drive in, there were still guardrails preventing drivers from going into traffic coming from the other direction and potentially causing a crash.

Your values and life themes are like guardrails in your life, and your commitment is essential to build and develop yourself as you move in your intentional direction, giving you the strength and courage to say no or yes with your choices and decisions. Famed Green Bay Packers head coach Vince Lombardi said, "The quality of a person's life is in direct proportion to their commitment to excellence, regardless of their chosen field of endeavor." You have the freedom to choose which lane to drive in, but commitment keeps you focused on the direction and path you are driving. Commitment is key, and it gives you confidence in your decisions.

Personal Responsibility and Ownership

When I was sixteen, I came home at about two a.m. early one Saturday morning. I had been out with friends, and usually, my parents were asleep when I got home late on the weekends. This time I was out a little later than usual, and for whatever reason, my dad was still up.

Well, the ensuing conversation went as well as you could imagine at two a.m. with a cocky, arrogant, and tired teenager and his father as we dialogued about responsibility, the possible trouble you can get into late at night, and a myriad of other actions that could derail my life and dreams as an athlete and human. After the back and forth with nothing really coming from the conversation, my dad stopped speaking, and a calm came across his face. He looked me in the eyes and said, "I trust you." With those words, he turned around, went back upstairs, and went to bed. That night was a turning point for me and my life.

One of the most discussed Jewish victims of the Holocaust, Anne Frank, shared this idea in her famed diary. "Parents can only give good advice or put them on the right paths, but the final forming of a person's character lies in their own hands." When my dad said those words— "I trust you"—something inside of me shifted, and that night, I took ownership of my choices and life!

I realized I had a choice in the direction my life would take. The decision wasn't going to be my father's, my coach's, friends', or anyone else. What smacked me in the face was that I was responsible for me, my life, my choices, and my attitude. My dream was to be the best soccer player ever to come from my small Michigan city where soccer was an afterthought, the economy was driven by agriculture, and football and basketball at the local university were the sports everyone focused on throughout the year.

If I wanted to be successful and achieve my goal, I had to be the one driving the process. I had to own my actions and decisions. No one was going to push me harder, farther, and faster than myself. I had to take ownership of my athletic success. Leadership expert John Maxwell reiterates this reality. "The greatest day in your life and mine is when we take total responsibility for our attitudes. That's the day we truly grow up." I took responsibility for my athletic career, and I choose to be willing to sacrifice and do what was necessary to see that dream come to a reality!

Get SMART

You don't have enough time, energy, or capacity to do everything. Imagining the future and putting your goals in focus gives you the power and clarity to say no. There is so much freedom in that simple word—*no*. Balance is essential to lasting success in sport and life. Over the past three chapters, we have examined three principles that will give you the *Focus* needed and give clarity to your future. Starting with the end in Mind Revisited, define what success means for you, and the power of your *no*.

It's now time to put into practice those principles and directly apply them to your life. One of the first steps in making the commitment to take responsibility and ownership of your current reality is through setting goals, having targets to aim at, to zero in on, and move toward. It takes effort and focus to think about your life and what life after your sport and competition will look like. Now you have the opportunity to put into action your commitment through SMART goals. Basically, goals give you a target to aim at and bring to life, and they give clarity to what success looks like for you.

Whenever that day comes for you to walk away from competing is when life after sport begins. As an athlete, you can go into a myriad of directions: coaching, start your own company, real estate, financial industry, and the list goes on. You are going to use the SMART goal framework to assist you with writing down your goals. SMART goals will help you continue to grow and find success today and as you move into your next career, clarifying your target and desired outcomes.

Let's break down SMART goals.

S—Specific—writing goals that are relevant, unique for you, state what you will do, and tell you how you know you have been successful.

M—Motivating—you are passionate about it, attach an emotion to the goal, connect to your *why*, and exciting to you!

A—Actionable—realistic to you and within your scope of possibility, use action words to describe, realistic and achievable.

R—Risky—not too easy, which leads to boredom, and not too difficult, which can lead to discouragement and/or demoralization. Challenge yourself and push your limits.

T—Trackable—give a specific date and/or deadline, provide a way to evaluate, have data targets and milestones leading to accomplishment.

Here are a few sample goals to help you think about setting your goals.

Finish the six classes needed to complete my bachelor's degree in communication and marketing in twenty-four months.

SMART Framework

Specific—Finish my degree.

Motivating—Feel joy to finish my degree and prepare me for working with a marketing firm after retirement.

Actionable—action verb—*finish* and realistic to complete in 24-month time frame.

Risky—Will need to work hard to complete in twenty-four months. Will need to take two classes during one of the six terms.

Trackable—Have a twenty-four-month deadline to complete and can evaluate at the end of each school term.

Start internship with local financial firm by November 14th to complete it during the two-month off-season.

SMART Framework

Specific—Start internship by November 14th.

Motivating—Feel excited to learn about and start internship and prepare for financial career.

Actionable—action verb—*start* and realistic to complete during the two-month off-season.

Risky—Will need to start by connecting with local financial firms; will need to initiate conversations within my network about opportunities.

Trackable—Start date of November 14th and duration of time available; two months during the off-season.

Keep Your Focus on What Matters

The beauty of the three principles of Focus—start with the end in mind revisited, clarify what success means for you and the power of your *no*— is that they act like a compass. They will guide you toward your true north, your destination. You may get pushed off course here or there or experience a dead end, but you will always be able to reorient yourself toward your destination by starting with the end in mind revisited, by clarifying what success means for you, and by finding balance through the power of your *no*.

Your ability to focus as an athlete is vital to your athletic success as well as to how well you transition to life after sport. By applying the Three Principles to Gaining Focus, you will have confidence as you go after your SMART Goals and navigate any transition. Even when you experience bumps, obstacles, and difficulties along the way, *Focus* will eliminate the distractions around you and the commitment to keep moving forward.

PART 5
TAKE ACTION

Action is the foundational key to all success.

—Pablo Picasso

You may be saying, "Jonathan, I have plenty of time to prepare for life after sport. There is no rush; I am good! My plan is to play for another two to three years, and then after that I will take some time and think about what I will do after I'm done." But is time on your side?

Let's take a quick look at the averages in professional sport. The reality is that professional careers are short and don't last that long! The average lengths of pro careers in the five major professional leagues in the US:

NFL: 3.5 years
NHL: 5.5 years
MLB: 5.6 years
NBA: 4.8 years
MLS: 3.2 years[24]

You may be in your rookie season or your first year of university, and the thought, let alone the idea, of preparing for your next career seems crazy. It could possibly be the furthest thing from your mind. You could also be toward the end of your career or somewhere in the middle, and you might be saying to yourself, "I will start thinking about all of this stuff after I retire." The harsh reality is that at some point, your career will end. Even the greatest professional athletes finish their careers at some point, and most don't have the luxury of finishing on their terms. Even if you have a long and successful career, you will be done with competing in your sport in your mid-thirties, with so much of your life ahead of you.

Have you ever thought about making repairs on your roof, a pipe in your house, your car, or something else? One of the more frustrating aspects of owning a car or a house is that they work—until they don't. There is required regular maintenance on a vehicle and home, but eventually, the vehicle or something in the house will break down. John F. Kennedy said, "The time to repair the roof is when the sun is shining." Trying to fix a leaking roof when it's raining outside is not enjoyable or easy. It is much easier to fix it when the sun is out and the pressure of repairing the roof isn't on so your things inside don't get ruined. Well, the sun is shining now on your life and career, and it is the time to prepare for life after sport.

No matter where you are in your playing career, whether it's your athletic career or your next career, you are the one who needs to take action, or someone else will decide for you. You have the choice now as you are competing as well as whenever your next career begins. So, I am challenging and imploring you to take ownership of your life and for what's to come.

Transition is not the easiest of experiences. It has ups and downs, struggles and triumphs, and obstacles and opportunities, but whenever you experience the mountain tops or the valleys of life, when you are prepared for those moments of transition, you will have confidence, courage, and grit to navigate through them.

In this last section of *SHIFT*, you will begin to work through the practical application of the framework. *Take Action* is when you collectively take all of what you have put together and begin to apply it every day. As athletes, we don't wait for other people to tell us when or how to take action. To be successful in sport, you initiate the contact, you take it to your opponent, and you take action. For life, it is the same perspective; take the next best step forward, write your story, and *Take Action*!

CHAPTER 13
ROW, ROW, ROW YOUR BOAT!

The price of greatness is responsibility.

—Winston Churchill

Can you envision standing on the podium with a gold medal around your neck, the national anthem playing, as your nation's flag is raised? That is a dream and vision for so many athletes. I can remember countless times watching the ceremony of athletes receiving their medals, tears running down their faces, and hearts filled with joy and satisfaction of success and representing their country in sport and competition.

I recently read the book *Boys in the Boat* by Daniel James Brown, which shed light on a sport, eight-man rowing, that I truly didn't know much about until I read the book.[25] Brown shares the story of nine working-class boys and their powerful stories of resilience, sacrifice, perseverance, and fortitude that culminated in overcoming the odds to beat Germany and Italy in the 1936 Olympics and win the gold medal.

The chips were stacked against them. They didn't come from privilege like many of the elites of rowing from the east coast at the time. They didn't have the history of rowing like Cambridge and Oxford in England or the resources from a dictator, in Adolf Hitler, working to prove to the world his dominance and superiority. Those nine boys overcame innumerable personal odds, navigating through the Great Depression, obstacles in the sport, and the reality of limited resources at the University of Washington, as well as internal struggles of depression, doubt, and the negative voices that all athletes experience throughout their careers and life.

The strength, fortitude, and speed for an eight-man rowing team to be successful is the collective unison and timing needed as each athlete rows simultaneously with power, pace, and timing. In any sport, there is beauty when it is performed with excellence; all eight rowing in sync, gliding across the water as if everyone is connected from head to toe. Their oars slip into the water, and with each powerful stroke, the boat moves at a blistering pace toward the finish line.

Each rower uses an oar that is attached to the boat by a pivot point called an oarlock or a thole. The oar, which is "a long shaft with a broad blade at the end, used for water propulsion or steering a boat,"[26] is used to row as the boat moves across the water. What's amazing in rowing is the beauty in its simplicity, while at the same time there is complexity to compete and perform with excellence.

At the end of the day, each athlete has an OAR that is used to propel them through competition, sport, and ultimately life. In the last step in the *SHIFT* framework,

Take Action, you have an OAR that propels and steers you as you navigate and move through life.

O—Ownership
A—Accountability
R—Responsibility

Ownership

Early in this book, you took a look at your story and began to remember what has shaped, impacted, and influenced your life, but what about moving forward? Remember, if you don't write your story, someone will write it for you. Your life and story are worth writing, be proactive; you have the power to be the author of your life!

In *Take Action*, you need to understand that today is the first step of the rest of your life, and it starts with you taking ownership. Own your life, your choices and decisions, and the trajectory and direction you are headed! You have put in solid work over the years in your sport. You have sacrificed, focused, zeroed in on, and pushed through; however, at some point, you will come to a place where the game is gone. You will no longer be competing. But your life is far from over; it is only beginning. Each new day is the first day for the rest of your life, so make it count—take action!

> "The best way to predict the future is to create it."
> —Abraham Lincoln

The sixteenth President of the United States, Abraham Lincoln, was attributed as saying, "The best way to predict the future is to create it." So, what will you create today, and what will you begin to create after you are done competing? The choice is yours. You are responsible for making it happen because no one else will create what's best for you.

Let's put this into a more relevant perspective. Would you ever allow others to control, dictate, or tell you how to find athletic success? Would you let someone else make your decisions on training, practice, nutrition, recovery, finances, relationships, work-life balance, or anything else that is needed to be successful as an athlete? No! Talent only gets you so far, and the truth is your work ethic, determination, focus, and grit are what gives you the opportunity to compete at the highest level in your sport. You made a choice to compete and sacrifice. Kobe Bryant once stated, "If you want to be great at something, there's a choice you have to make. What I mean by that is, there are inherent sacrifices that come along with that. Family time, hanging out with friends, being a great friend, being a great son, nephew, whatever the case may be." When thinking about ownership, the first thought for me that comes to mind is a house or car. You might be thinking you can also rent an apartment or house, and you can rent a car. But the reality is that at some point, you have to return the vehicle and the apartment or house. It is not yours; it is owned by someone else.

I remember when we moved into our first home. Rachel and I had been married for a few years. We signed the paperwork, got the keys, and drove to our new home. We walked up to the front door, unlocked it, and walked into the house. It was ours! We took ownership of that house on that day. It was an amazing feeling. Other than being surprised that we owned the house, there was one other tiny detail. For us to continue to own the house, we had to make these monthly payments to the bank to maintain ownership. If we decided to stop making those payments, we would eventually lose ownership of the house and no longer be able to live there. In addition, we had to maintain the house, keep it clean, and make repairs as well as updates. Because we owned the house, it was up to us to make it happen.

Life is much the same. You own your life and the decisions you make each day. If you stop making those decisions, or *payments*, someone or something else will step in and start making those payments for you. The problem, though, is they will also take *ownership* of you. You will give over the power you have in your life to someone or something else. I don't know about you, but I don't want someone else to write my story, my hope and my desire are to pen it myself. I hope you have that same dream!

Just as a physical oar propels the boat and rower through the water, Ownership is essential to propel and steer you through your life, sport, and competition. Don't give your ownership away to someone else so they determine your path and direction. Write your story, and own it!

Accountability

An oar can be used to propel you through the water as well as steer you by directing, redirecting, and setting a course of direction for your boat. Accountability is like steering; it will redirect, adjust your course, keep you focused on your determined target, your finish line, or your goal. Accountability in your life is helping you steer through the chaos, the ups and downs and ebbs and flows that competition, sport, and life throw at you.

Let me clarify what Accountability is; it is when you are being held to account for your actions or inactions.

The seventeenth-century French playwright, poet, and actor Moliere said, "It is not only what we do, but also what we do not do, for which we are accountable." It is essential to own your mistakes, inaction, and failures as well as your successes. Being accountable is not about shame or guilt but about authenticity, development, growth, and competing and living to the best of your abilities. You need to recognize and understand the impact of your actions, but also your inaction or lack of action within the spaces, circumstances, and arenas you inhabit.

> "It is not only what we do, but also what we do not do, for which we are accountable."
> —Moliere

We have already dived into the importance of building up your team and the characteristics of who you want on your team. The power and impact in your life of accountability are directly affected by those closest to you—your *team*! The obvious mistakes are easy to identify. It is those actions or inactions that get called out by those who care about you and create significant moments of growth and change. Having the right people around you will show you grace and forgiveness but also will speak the hard truth when needed to correct and realign your trajectory.

One quick thought to challenge you before you move any further. How do you currently feel or experience accountability? When confronted, does your body tense up, your heart rate increase, or do you clench your fists? Does your mind go to a memory when accountability was abused or misused to profit or benefit someone else at your expense? I realize everyone comes to the table with different experiences, biases, and perspectives; moreover, specific words or ideas can carry different weights for different people, but before we move forward, I want to challenge you to see accountability through a positive lens or filter.

When you can only see the first step, you still need to take it. Remember, a journey of a thousand miles begins with the first step. Don't be afraid to take risks and allow your journey and life's GPS to reroute itself. I know we mentioned this previously, but it is important to reiterate here. When you are using Google Maps, Apple Maps, or a GPS device and take a wrong turn or miss your turn, you are rerouted to the next best possible route to reach your destination. Sometimes you backtrack, but other times you are given a new route to help you get back on track. How does this apply to accountability? Take this principle and apply it to your life. The next time you make a mistake or take a wrong turn, whether it be from your own recognition or from someone in your *team*, focus on rerouting, and take the next best step to get you back on track. The power of accountability will help guide you by rerouting, and it will keep moving you forward to take the next right step forward in life. Simon Sinek shares the importance of having a *team* around you to keep you accountable. "Give someone responsibility and they will do their best. Make them accountable and they will do even better."

Accountability is like your personal GPS guiding, directing, and rerouting as you navigate life. What's amazing is you have the choice of how impactful and influential accountability is used in your life. You have the power to clarify the settings of accountability to create guardrails for yourself. The right settings can help you identify the shortest routes, the fastest routes, hear a female voice, a British accent, always avoid toll roads, etc. You get the idea. Remember, you are writing your story, and accountability is how you create your narrative. When you build your team, you are putting together the settings on your life, and accountability is the process you navigate and journey along as you pursue your goals, experiences, achieve accomplishments, develop, and grow. Accountability is key!

Responsibility

When you take action, you are the one making those decisions and sacrifices, not someone else. You have made the choice to compete, and you have taken personal responsibility to say yes to your sport and achieve the highest possible level of competition available to you. That same resolve, determination, and focus are needed in whatever arena you compete in next. The playwright George Bernard Shaw said, "We are made wise not by the recollection of our past, but by the responsibility for our future." That same intentionality is needed across your life. You can't change what has already taken place or the present, but you can create your future. It is your choice on what you do, what decisions you make, and what mindset you adopt as you move forward.

There is an old adage my dad would say when I was growing up. "You can lead a horse to water, but you can't make it drink." This saying is true not only for animals but also for people—regardless of the opportunity, task, hurdle, obstacle, or goal that's in front of you. You have to choose whether or not to go over, under, through it, or run away from it. Other people can bring the issue or problem or opportunity to you, but you have to take responsibility and make the choice whether or not you take action. So, the question on the table for you now is, will you take responsibility for your life?

Where do you start?

How will you develop personal responsibility?

Four Essential Truths about Personal Responsibility

1. *You have a choice on whether or not you take responsibility.* You have the choice to allow someone or something else to determine your path and direction. You have settled into whatever space you are in, and you are okay with where you are at in the world and the people around you. To take responsibility, you first need to choose whether or not to do so. So, I am asking you right now, will you accept responsibility for yourself, your thoughts, actions, decisions, and growth? This is your first step, either take responsibility or give your power over to someone else!

2. *To learn from your mistakes, you have to own them.* The idea and the pursuit of perfection are unattainable. You can compete with excellence, but perfection will not become a reality for you as an athlete, let alone as a human. We are finite, and mistakes are part of life, but your perspective drastically affects how you experience mistakes and how you navigate through them. Dr. Carol Dweck spoke on this at a TED talk in 2014. She highlighted the importance and idea of *the not yet.*[27] Your present reality doesn't define you. You can shape your future self and strive and work to pursue what your future self will look like. You are not there yet, but you are making progress toward that future. Take risks and be okay with mistakes, learn from them and keep going!

3. *You can't rest on your victories.* I remember running across the finish line in the 200 meters early in my track career; it was an amazing feeling to

be first. I put my heart and soul into that race, didn't hold anything back, and left everything on the course. My legs were like Jello®, my heart was pounding, and I could barely catch my breath—I had won. The only issue was I then realized that race was only the first heat. There were three more heats and then a final race to determine the winner. It was my first track meet, and I was devastated in that moment. I didn't know how track meets are organized. The principle I learned that day is still true today; because you win doesn't mean you can stop. Enjoy the moment, but keep moving forward. Don't stop.

It feels great to hold the trophy and to be the champion, but eventually, someone else will be crowned and deemed the winner, someone else will be on the top of the podium, and the records will be broken. That's okay! The real problem arises when you stop growing and developing. Earlier in the book, we addressed success and what success is and how you define it. Taking responsibility for your definition is key to help you see yourself now as you compete, in the future, and what success will look like for you moving forward. It is a both/and, not an either/or. Don't focus and settle on your victories of your past; rather, highlight what your success is and your best will be in the future.

4. *Making excuses or blaming others is giving away your power.* Taking responsibility is taking an authentic look at your actions and those circumstances out of your control. When you blame someone or something else or make an excuse for why failure or a mistake occurred, what is

being communicated is the results, victories, loss, growth, and development is determined by whoever is being blamed. You are, in essence, saying that for you to grow and improve and ultimately have success, whoever you are blaming needs to change, not you. Responsibility is about controlling what you can and not giving your power away to other people or outside forces.

When you make mistakes or when things don't go your way, it's easier to blame someone else or make excuses about why you didn't achieve your desired outcome.[28] There is a natural survivalist reaction that comes out when people fail or make mistakes that attempts to protect the individual. By passing the blame onto someone else, we feel better about ourselves, and we create a sense that the mistake is no longer our own fault. Don't fall into this trap! Merely because the feeling or emotion has passed doesn't equal growth and improvement. Take responsibility for your actions, learn from your mistakes, and grow!

You Are a Work in Progress

Take Action means you are culminating all of the work you have put in thus far, putting that work into bite-size chunks, and creating actions that you can start today. These actions will move you one step closer to success and lead you toward accomplishing your goals tomorrow. Remember that Winston Churchill said, "The price of greatness is responsibility." Greatness is found not in the trophies or awards you have won, but in the life you live as an athlete and beyond. As you move closer to life after sport, or if you are already there, you are the one who needs to take ownership, create accountability, and have personal responsibility for your life, choices, actions, spirituality, and mentality to navigate the present and future.

You have already demonstrated Ownership, Accountability, and Responsibility (OAR) as an athlete; you wouldn't have found success if you hadn't. As you navigate through life by taking hold of your OAR, you will experience propulsion as you steer through the waters of life. You can't achieve it all in a moment. Accomplishing goals and achieving athletic success takes time, hard work, character, clarity, goals, grit, and sacrifice. The same is true for you and a healthy and successful transition to life after sport—whenever that day arrives. It is up to you, and nobody else can do it for you. To be successful now and in the future, you need to grab your OAR and prepare for whatever your next step in life and career may be. You've got this. *Take Action* today!

CHAPTER 14
WHAT IS TRULY HOLDING YOU BACK?

Whether you think you can,
or think you can't, you're right.

—Henry Ford

"Shut up and dribble," #morethananathlete, #BLM, kneeling, and many other hashtags, statements, movements, and mantras have been at the forefront of sport over the past few years. There has been a broader movement toward recognition, realization, and actualization that, as an athlete, you have a platform and a voice beyond your sport. Now is the time to stand up, verbalize injustice, and dialogue about the problem(s) you want to help solve and be part of the solution rather than continue to sit on the bench.

But why now?

What is it about 2019 and 2020 that athletes are now finding their voices and the confidence to speak up and speak out for injustice across multiple sports' competitions? Why the large number of athletes taking a stand or, better said, kneeling? There are passions, desires for change, influence, and societal impact that are inside of you that are beyond your sport, personal branding, marketing, starting your company, and more that have been pushed to the forefront unlike any other time in our world. Athletes are speaking out.

When I first began working and mentoring professional soccer players, it was a different time. Over a decade ago, athletes didn't speak out about injustice to the extent or the breadth they do today. To be honest, athletes didn't talk about much more than their sport, the results, their contracts, teammates, or the teams they are competing for or against. There were a few exceptions, but those were limited. It was almost taboo, and if you brought up issues or desire for change, that took your focus away from your sport, which was a bad thing and unprofessional! I'm curious; what do you think has changed for the better to give athletes the confidence to speak up and speak out, do more than only compete, and be part of the solution?

It is interesting how you can hear a lie, a falsehood told to you for so long, yet, because it is repeated over and over again, you start to believe it. More often than not, limiting beliefs are such ideas, thoughts, and falsehoods. Limiting beliefs are part of the broader spectrum of beliefs that you hold to be true and are grounded in fact as well as life experience and emotion. For the most part, they are created or developed in our youth. Amy Morin, author of *13 Things Mentally Strong People Don't Do*, shares three types of unhealthy self-limiting beliefs: unhealthy beliefs about yourself, unhealthy beliefs about others, and unhealthy beliefs about the world.[29]

As you think back to *Start Now*, recall the importance of remembering your story and the moments along the way that helped shaped your beliefs. We all establish or make up limiting beliefs because that is what we were told, or we create those beliefs to protect ourselves based on past experiences. Those beliefs hold you back or limit you from developing and holding an accurate and true view of yourself, others, and the world, even though the belief was created in your mind to protect you. That is one of the responsibilities your brain has for you—to survive and keep you safe. So, over time you have created beliefs that your brain tells you are there to protect you from danger, and those beliefs are not limited to one area or aspect of your life. They are triggered when your brain thinks you are in danger.

Uncovering Limiting Beliefs

As an athlete, your sport was your haven, your safe space, the time when you felt alive or at your best. It was also the space where others praised you, you got noticed, others liked you, you felt valued and important. It is no wonder so much of the sport and identity as an athlete is tied into our thoughts and personal beliefs.

When we are young and playing a game, not much else matters, or at least, not much else matters as much. The safety and affirmation sport and competition brought into your life felt good on multiple levels, and beliefs about sport and competition were developed in your mind.

"The only thing that's keeping you from getting what you want is the story you keep telling yourself."
—Tony Robbins

What story have you been telling yourself? What's the narrative that has been running through your conscience and mind from an early age? What beliefs do you believe and hold as truth that are holding you back and limiting what you think you are capable of in and outside of sport? Tony Robbins once said, "The only thing that's keeping you from getting what you want is the story you keep telling yourself." We are going to focus on the narrative and story you are telling yourself and work to rewrite your thinking and turn those limiting beliefs into positive truths about who you are to get to where you want to go.

The majority of your beliefs are developed early on in your life from life circumstances and from those who are influential in your life, such as your parents, grandparents, coaches, extended family, and peers.[30] For the most part, your beliefs have served you well up until this point. The power, impact, and opportunity sport give you are amazing. A lot of my youth was spent playing, competing, and enjoying sport. I am making an educated guess that your childhood was much the same—sport was an integral part of your life. Your sport(s) became a focus and space where you developed your identity and belief about yourself, others, and the world. I know I did. And many of my beliefs were developed through my parents, coaches, and peers within that environment.

Regardless of how confident and secure you were as an athlete and your sport, there were also limiting beliefs developed during these formative years. When thinking about those limiting beliefs, you may not recognize all of them now, but there will come a day when you bump up against those beliefs. When your beliefs were developed, they focused on sport and your involvement in those athletic opportunities. One of the key questions you have to ask yourself is, "What happens when those opportunities, your sport, are no longer available?" What happens when you are no longer able to walk into a locker room or onto a court or field and when no coach is encouraging you, helping, guiding, or inspiring as you compete? Where do you go with your beliefs then? Each season I have worked with elite athletes, at least one will say something along the lines of, "I am an athlete, and that is all I know. I don't have any other passions or know about anything else. My sport is all there is for me." Does that sound familiar? Are those words or something similar the same you hear yourself saying as well?

In this fifth step, *Take Action*, you are exploring the beliefs you have internalized for years, even to the point where you don't even recognize you have them. Whether or not you realize it, those beliefs are holding you back and preventing you from taking risks and exploring other options out in the world. As a quick reminder, your beliefs are often what help protect you. They are not bad, but they will limit what you are capable of doing and accomplishing, and that is why you need to address the limiting beliefs in your life.

Win or go home! That was the motto on the playground where I grew up playing basketball. It was a survival of the fittest type of mentality. If you could play, you played. If you couldn't, then you sat and watched. Because your brain desires for you to survive, you stand and "ball out," or you leave, but there comes a point in your life when what you believe is holding you back from where you want to go. If you don't want to stay where you are, you have to keep moving forward. You are more than your sport, greater than your competition, and more influential than what you can do in between the lines. Your life and our world need you beyond the sport, and your contribution to impact your sphere of influence is needed more than ever before. The question for you today is, do you truly believe that?

I do!

What's Playing on Repeat in Your Mind?

When you repeat those limiting beliefs to yourself, you get derailed, knocked off course, and you settle for wherever you are at. You fall back into destructive or poor habits: binge-watching Netflix, useless activities that add no value to your life or others, scrolling mindlessly through social media apps, alcohol or drugs, and a multitude of other things. One easy indicator of these negative habits is to look back at your activities and efforts and see whether or not your time, talent, and treasure was wasted. Did the time investment add value to your life or others' lives?

You would never settle on the field or in competition, and you wouldn't waste your time and energy on activities and things that add no value to your athletic success. So why settle or be okay with settling in other aspects of your life? Part of the reason why you settle is the limiting beliefs you have agreed with, bought into, and made part of your self-talk, thought process, and identity.

To help you start identifying the limiting beliefs in your life, I have written a few common limiting beliefs I have heard from athletes over the years.

Examples

"I will worry and plan for retirement after I'm done playing; I have plenty of time."

"I am an introvert, so it's hard to connect with others and network."

"It doesn't matter if I prepare for life after sport or not; it will all work itself out."

"All I know is my sport; I have nothing else to offer."

"My sport is what makes me valuable and significant. Without my sport, I'm nothing."

"I'm a pro athlete. There will be people lined up to offer me a job when I'm done playing."

"I will play and have an amazing career and will make enough money, so I don't have to worry about what's next."

Do any of these sound familiar? Maybe as you read through that list, a few of your own beliefs or thoughts came to mind. What do you do with these limiting beliefs, and how do you combat them? They will not go away easily; they have been ingrained into your life, mind, sub-conscience, and mentality. Even if you don't believe them outright, they have contributed to where you are emotionally, physically, psychologically, spiritually, and intellectually in your development and mindset.

The 6-R Cycle

The difficulty of navigating limiting beliefs is the unhealthy thought process and habits that have developed as a result of them. To help guide you through overcoming your limiting beliefs, I have created a six-step process that will help you identify the limiting beliefs in your life, replace them with new beliefs about who you are (your best self), strengthen your new beliefs, and build upon them as you continue to move forward as you grow in self-awareness and navigate new territory in this world!

1. Recognize

The first step for identifying a limiting belief is to recognize it. This is not an easy task, as you average around 6,200 thoughts every day. Even though your thoughts may seem disjointed, there are connection points throughout the thought process in your brains.[31] Similar to training physically, you will have to start training mentally as you begin to examine what you are telling yourself throughout the day as you interact with your environment. Here are few questions to help you explore thoughts and ideas about life after playing.

What do you feel when something negative or positive occurs?

What emotions come up when talking about life after sport or the thought of not playing any longer?

How do you respond when you hear stories about former teammates or other athletes who were forced to retire due to injury or some other unfair circumstance?

How do you view yourself outside of your sport?

You may experience a trigger that brings up an emotion and a limiting belief, so look for those moments and be self-aware to recognize the change in your emotional state, how your body reacts physically, the thought or idea that occurred, or a specific belief that came to mind as you thought about those questions. You can't move forward unless you first recognize the limiting belief, so take the time to reflect and assess your thoughts. Similar to when you have been assessed as an athlete at a try-out or evaluation, you are assessing the ideas and thoughts that come to mind when you encounter the reality of life after sport, transition, or even at a basic level of stressful moments or interactions. The first and most important step is to recognize the limiting belief.

2. Reject

The Greek word *metanoia* means a *change of mind*, and it implies making an intentional decision to turn around and face a new direction. When you reject the limiting beliefs in your life, that is exactly what you are doing. You are making an intentional decision to turn around and face a new direction by believing a new truth about who you are or what you can accomplish. It is not enough simply to try to ignore it because the idea and the belief are still present; ignoring it would be like turning your back on someone in a room and then believing they are no longer there because you can't see them. There is an intentional act to reject the identified limiting belief.

First, recognize the limiting belief, then reject it by remembering the power of your *no*. You are moving in a new direction and intentionally turning away from the limiting belief by rejecting it and moving in a new direction.

3. Replace

This is where the new belief about self, others, or your world comes into play. Now that you have recognized the limiting belief and you have rejected the limiting belief, you now have space to place a new, healthy truth and direction about yourself. Rather than, "My sport is what makes me valuable and significant," you can say, "My value is based on my humanity, and sport is the opportunity to display what I can do." Here is the thing; you must replace the old belief with a new one. Otherwise, the limiting belief will refill the void. Once you reject the old limiting belief, there is a gap now in its space that needs to be filled, so fill it with a truth about yourself. If you do nothing, the gap will be refilled with the old, limiting belief.

When you have an experience, your thoughts respond to that experience through a past memory and an emotion that has created and established the limiting belief. Now that you are rejecting the limiting belief that usually comes to mind in that specific experience, you have to replace it with a new belief. Otherwise, your old, limiting belief will return to its space, similar to how you develop new athletic technique or habits. To try and change your shooting technique or your swing, you have to replace the old with something new. This same principle is true with your beliefs. Replace it, or you will revert back to what you have historically done or thought.

Pit Stop

Now that you have recognized, rejected, and replaced your limiting belief, we are going to take a quick *pit stop*. In sport and moments in time, we have these periods of struggle or difficulty; it's normal. Whether it's during the dog days of summer or working through the grind of a long season, every athlete experiences moments each season that could be called the *messy middle*.[32]

You have identified the limiting belief, rejected it, and created space to replace it. You have this new true belief about who you are and what you can accomplish that you are working toward adopting and internalizing, but then life, unknowns, other people, or even the old limiting beliefs come crashing in around you to wreak havoc on your life. No matter how hard you try, the *messy middle* will rear its ugly face somehow, some way, but keep going. Don't stop moving forward. One of the reasons we don't stop after the third step is because of the *messy middle*. To cement and strengthen your foundation and move into the growth and success that is waiting for you on the other side of the *messy middle*, you have to navigate through the next three steps.

4.   Remind

I remember my first year of playing competitive basketball. Up until this point, I only played pick-up on the playground. I was given a playbook with ten plays for a motion offense and a number of different out-of-bounds plays. At first, I was surprised. I wasn't sure what to do and was a little confused. I thought, "Why do we have plays? You show up and compete and beat your opponent by scoring more points." Well, I took the new playbook home and started to learn the plays. To make things a little more difficult, I had to learn multiple positions, their roles, and the movements for the plays depending on which position I was in at the time. Eventually, I learned the plays, ran through them in my mind to visualize, and practiced with my teammates.

To make your new belief stick, you have to remind yourself continually of the new belief. Like I had to commit to memory my playbook, so you also need to put your new belief to memory, and you do that by reminding yourself of the new belief. That comes through a two-step process of remembering and reflecting.

It takes time, and sometimes the new belief won't stay in place. It will take practice as you remind yourself of the new belief about yourself. You are rewiring your brain and thought process as you experience life. To remember what your new belief is before you internalize it, you will work at reminding yourself of your new belief, like I reminded myself of the playbook I received for basketball. One easy, simple way to remind yourself is to write out your new belief statements. This practice will give you the opportunity to reflect on the new belief, commit it to memory, and have a visible reminder. You can take this practice one step further by including those in your *team* to help by assisting in reminding you about your new belief. Remember, "To go far, go together!"

5. Reinforce

To build up and give great strength is essential as you move through these steps. Be intentional to build a stronghold around your new belief in your mind through your self-talk, meditation, mindfulness, and actions. Let's revisit the process to learn a new technique or move. If you don't focus in on the new technique or way of movement, you will naturally fall back into your old habit and technique. To learn something new, you will have to focus on the new movement and practice it repeatedly, reinforcing the movement until it becomes a natural part of how you move. This same principle is true with your new true belief. You will work toward developing and building your new true belief and by reinforcing it, which will help you prevent the old limiting belief from coming back into your mind and heart and taking root again.

What's important here is to reinforce your new belief through practice and repetition. You got to get those reps! Work through this trigger and thought process to reinforce your new belief. "If I think—(limiting belief),—press pause—recognize, reject, replace and think your—(new belief)." Remember the thought progress: you experience an event, you remember a memory and feel an emotion, then you respond with action. This process doesn't take long, but it impacts your life multiple times throughout the day. The power of reinforcing your new belief through a trigger and response can be accomplished by meditating on your new belief. That will reinforce the new belief about yourself. So, when you have the experience and feel the emotion, rather than focusing on the limiting belief, you remember and focus on your new true belief about your best self.

Patience throughout this process will help guide you. Learning a new skill or a new playbook takes time, so will the practice of reinforcing your new belief. You don't think about it once, and you are good to go. Similarly, you don't run a new play and simply know it and how to run it in a game situation. It takes time, but it is invaluable as you learn the new process to recognize, reject, replace, remind, and reinforce your new belief.

6. Repeat

The final step in the *Six R* process is to Repeat as necessary. The reality is you can't tackle all of your limiting beliefs at once. Focusing in on one or two at a time is a good place to start because it can get overwhelming and feel like you are being pulled in multiple directions. As you mature and grow, you will begin to realize you have many limiting beliefs about yourself, others, and the world. The pursuit of your best true self is a life-long pursuit and journey as you develop, grow in your self-awareness, and become who you are created to be. As you practice and get repetitions and games, you will improve and grow in your experience with this process. Over time, you will hone your skills with the *Six R's* and the process will take mere seconds to navigate through and process. Similarly, as you practice plays multiple times over and over, you don't need to think about the play because you have practiced and prepared; you simply act and do.

What is amazing is that you will create growth and momentum as you navigate through this process and replace your limiting beliefs with true beliefs about yourself. Building up your playbook or making additions to a playbook or set plays as the season goes on, you will also begin to see limiting beliefs in other areas of your life that you didn't recognize previously. You are fully connected as a human, and each area or aspect of your life overlaps into other areas and aspects. So, as you work through the *Six R* process, you will begin to see opportunities for growth in areas other than within your sport. These opportunities will affect all aspects of your life beyond competition and the sport you play as you pursue living at your best holistically.

Don't allow the limiting beliefs in your life to derail and hold you back from being who you have been created to be. The *Six R* process to overcome limiting beliefs will guide you through the process of becoming your true best self. As you Recognize the limiting belief,

Reject it, and Replace it with a new belief about your best self. Remind yourself through Remembering and Reflecting. Reinforce your new belief about your best self through meditation and thought processes, and finally, Repeat as you begin to observe and experience other limiting beliefs.

Your life is a journey, and each day is the next step as you move forward. A journey of a thousand miles begins with a single step, and today is your first step. The playbook has been given to you, and now it's time to put in the work to learn, grow, and develop. Each day you have a choice on what you do and whether or not you move closer to your best self and what you have been destined to accomplish and live out—not only in sport but, more importantly, in life.

Transition is not easy, but it is guaranteed. No matter how passionate and focused you are on your sport, the game will eventually end for you whether or not you are prepared. You have been given this amazing gift of life that is greater than your sport. I know that may sound crazy right now, but it's true. You have an amazing life beyond the game and many years to experience life to its fullest and all it has in store for you. Who you are is not defined by the score, stats, or data that measures what you do; you are more than an athlete, and now it's time to start believing that! Don't allow the limiting beliefs to hold you back from accomplishing all that you have been destined to accomplish!

CHAPTER 15

WHY THE BEST IDEAS COME TO MIND IN THE SHOWER

People don't decide their future, they decide
their habits and their habits decide their future.

—F. Matthias Alexander

Where do you get your best ideas? Where do you find
those moments in time where all of a sudden, the heav-
ens open up, and you have this revelation, an epiphany,
or breakthrough. I'm not sure if you have ever experienced this, but for me, it's in the shower. I know that
may sound funny or weird, but some of the best ideas
I have ever had came to me when I was getting clean.
Those light bulb moments pushed me to ask why?
Why then and there? What was it about the time in
the shower? Wow, that sounds a little ridiculous when
I typed it. Anyway, what I discovered was the shower
wasn't an amazing space, but it was actually the reality

that my mind didn't have to focus on anything specific while I washed my hair or body. Because I have taken thousands of showers, my movements are on autopilot. I don't have to think about them. Therefore, my mind is able to wander and be free to think about anything and everything, and it is at those moments that thoughts, ideas, and insights come flooding into my brain. This same reality is true for brushing your teeth and other activities where your body is put on autopilot. You don't have to think about the movement of brushing, and your mind and thoughts wander.

You might be asking, "So what? What does this have to with the last step in the *SHIFT* framework and this book?" Well, what comes to mind or what do you think of when you hear the phrase, *Take Action?* For me, there is an immediate response. I think I need to do something, RIGHT NOW, whether it is making a decision, a choice, an act, or some form of initiative. What it doesn't mean to me is to wait or be passive or dismissive about what's going on, but here is a little secret: taking action all the time is not realistic or feasible in our life or current spaces.

And that's okay!

So far, you have worked hard to get where you are today—in life and as you have navigated through this book. If some of your best insights have been sparked when your mind is at rest or not needing to use precious energy sources to think or process, what does it look like for you to create these magical moments intentionally each day?

The secret—routines and habits.

Research from Duke University has shown that 40 percent of our days are driven by habits.[33] How crazy is that? Forty percent! Those actions you do each day are part of your daily routine. You naturally do them each day because you repeatedly have to do them over and over until they have been hardwired into your brain. Have you ever thought about what your ideal day would look like? What would it look like if the day went the way you wanted it? What time would you wake up? What's your morning routine, your workday, your meals, evening time, and ideal bedtime? Now, the harder question is how close does your current daily life align with your ideal day? A simple exercise to help you with this is to track your day. Write down what you did in the morning, during the workday, and in the evening. After recording a few days, reflect on what you discovered. Then, go back and write out what your ideal day would look like.

Your daily habits are important to recognize in the present so that as you move forward and think about today and your future, you can be at your best. With habits driving so much of your daily life, you have to wonder whether they are good, bad, or indifferent? Are the actions you are taking each day building you up and helping you grow, or are they limiting you and holding you back from what you desire to achieve and accomplish?

In the previous chapter, we started to explore limiting beliefs and how to overcome the lies we have bought into and that have been created in our mindset and actions. Our habits will reinforce our limiting beliefs, so our focus in the previous chapter was to identify the limiting beliefs and replace them with truths about your best self. Then, we need to work to reinforce good and healthy beliefs that lead to a stronger growth mindset, develop grit, perseverance, endurance, and many other positive character skills.

James Clear, in his book *Atomic Habits*, emphasized this reality by stating that, "Progress requires unlearning.

Becoming the best version of yourself requires you to continuously edit your beliefs, and to upgrade and expand your identity." When you look back at the *SHIFT* framework, you have already put in significant work to become a version of your best self. You have clarified and answered questions about who you are and whose you are. You have identified your values and life themes. You have begun to dream about what could be and your future self, which is very difficult because it can be abstract to think about what your future self could be due to our focus on the present.

> "Progress requires unlearning. Becoming the best version of yourself requires you to continuously edit your beliefs, and to upgrade and expand your identity."
> —James Clear

I am proud of the work and time you have invested in yourself and how you will navigate through transitions in sport and to life after sport. Don't pull your foot off the gas yet, though. It is the final minutes of the game, the final play, the last turn. It's not over yet; keep going, finish it out, and finish strong.

Habits Create a Life

Have you ever been to the Grand Canyon or seen pictures of it? First off, pictures and images don't do it justice. It is majestic and awe-inspiring! As you step out toward the edge and look across the vast canyon, your breath is taken away—from the richness of colors throughout the various levels of soil and sediment; then as your eyes gravitate toward the bottom of the canyon to the Colorado River flowing through the rock, it is difficult to put it into words the collective beauty and grandness. Then you think of the time it took to be created. The days, weeks, months, and years of water flowing over those rocks and how the river slowly took away the sediment and eventually created this majestic work of art in nature.

Habits and routines are like the river flowing and creating the canyon. They are little actions that create big change and impact. Success, growth, and development happens daily, not in a day. Your daily choices directly impact your monthly and yearly success. Confucius said, "The man who moves a mountain begins by carrying away small stones." Be consistent and dedicated in moving those small rocks in your life. As you continue to move forward, you will realize the significant impact and changes that have taken place when you reflect on our progress.

As an athlete, you have used habits to help you prepare for training, practice, and games. You may also call these moments *pre-game routines*, or daily rituals or training preparation, but whatever you call them, they are a series of actions taken to help your body and mind zero in, focus on, and prepare for what's to come. Whether it is foam rolling, band work, a cup of coffee, how you go to sleep at night, or as simple as what you do as you walk into the locker room, all of these little actions are habits you have cultivated as an athlete to help you perform at your best. Author and speaker Steven Pressfield said, "The difference between an amateur and a professional is in their habits. An amateur has amateur habits. A professional has professional habits." You are an elite athlete performing at a high level. Doesn't it make sense to leverage that same mentality for your life, especially knowing that at some point, you will be required to stop competing? You may not be sure when that day may come, but it will arrive at some point, and my hope and desire is that you will be prepared for that moment so you can successfully navigate through it and seize the opportunity presented in that transition!

Habits Lead the Way

What does this have to do with transition to life after sport? In transition, if you are not prepared for it, it can negatively affect you. Think about transitions in sport: the turn in the pool for a swimmer, counterattack in soccer, double play in baseball, the baton handoff in track and field, the walk from the green to the next tee in golf. All of those moments of transition in sport are small moments that you prepare for significantly to maximize opportunity. Races are won in the handoff, goals are scored in the counterattack, one poor putt can lead to the next poor tee shot, and the list goes on. In all of those examples, time and practice are needed to be successful during those moments of transition, and the same is true for when you make the transition to life after sport. You must be prepared!

Over and over again, I have heard retired athletes say, "I wish I would have started sooner!" Recently, I was sitting across the table from Thomas, a former pro soccer player who has been retired for almost two years at this point. We were talking about his soccer camp business, marketing, branding, and what he was working toward over the next twelve months. About halfway through our conversation, he stopped, looked me in the eyes with frustration, and said, "I just thought all of this would be easier! I thought people would be lining up to give me a job or help me with my soccer camp business." What Thomas realized that morning and former athletes all over the world realize once they retire is that it's hard work, and whatever you decide to do after your professional career takes time, energy, effort, and focus—exactly like your pro career. Nothing worth investing in comes easily, and the things that are valuable and important will cost you something!

So start today. Take action. What will you start to do today to set yourself up for tomorrow? Our brains are constantly looking for ways to increase efficiency and cut out clutter, and habits and routines are a great way to do that. By intentionally creating routines in your daily activities and building good habits, you will not only continue to grow and develop day by day, but you are also establishing a foundation that will withstand the pressure, setbacks, and frustrations that life throws at you.

James Clear shares that "Habits are like the entrance ramp to a highway. They lead you down a path and, before you know it, you're speeding toward the next behavior." So, let's take action and create healthy habits that will set you up for success and put you on the highway moving toward your best true self and the behaviors you desire.

I was talking with Juan one afternoon about what has been a key to his longevity and success as a professional; he was going into his eleventh year playing professionally. He said without hesitation, "Great performances start the night before." He emphasized the importance of getting a good night of sleep, a solid ten hours, that would prepare his mind and body to perform at its peak in the game the next night. He then went onto describe in detail his morning routine, from wake-up to his breakfast, morning walk, his music list, lunch, afternoon nap, visualization prep, the route he takes to the stadium, how he walks into the locker room, pre-game routine, game performance, recovery, and then getting back in bed. What amazed me was the detail he gave as he described each step and why he chose it, the purpose behind the action, and his intentionality.

Habitually Design Your Ideal Day

I first heard the idea of creating an ideal day and week from Michael Hyatt and his teachings on productivity and efficiency. It is the practice that you write out what an ideal day looks like for you. As an athlete, what would the ideal day with training look like, and what would an ideal game day look like? Go into detail and describe your ideal day and week.

As you write all of this down, you are setting the standard and ideal environment you desire to be created for you to be at your best. Now, there is one simple caveat, and that is that life is life, and disruptions and stuff hit the fan at some points. That doesn't mean you can't have an ideal day in mind as you navigate chaos or uncertainty. The ideal day gives you clarity, direction, and focus when life does go sideways. It is like having a true north for each day, and even though life may throw you off course, your ideal day allows you to readjust and get back on course.

Take some time and write out your ideal day and ideal week. Be as descriptive as possible. Write down your morning routine, what actions you take to prepare for the day, what will allow you to be at your best, and what actions will lead to the next action. Map out the 24 hours of the day and seven days for the week, then fill in what ideally you desire to do during that time. Again, be as descriptive as possible.

Honing Your Habits

Now that you have your ideal day and ideal week, those are daily and weekly routines that will set you up for success. Let's take a closer look at your habits. Acknowledging that 40 percent of your day is based on habits, obviously, your habits have a significant impact on your life. There are sleeping habits, eating habits, relational habits, work habits, and athletic habits. The habits you have developed for your sport as an elite athlete have been honed and cultivated over time, and they actually transfer over into life beyond sport. The same things you have developed on a daily basis for training, practice, and game days will help you be successful off the field.

The question is, what are the specific habits that will add value for you and your life after sport? What are some of the actions you do to help or propel you to be successful in transition? If you think that there are no habits that cross over or possibly the habits you do have would potentially hold you back, it is okay. The ancient proverb shares, "The best time to plant a tree is twenty years ago, and the second best time is today." So, start today to establish and intentionally create healthy habits to be successful and transition to life after sports.

Regardless of what habits you currently have or what adjustments you want to make, your desire to start or modify a habit begins with a small, tiny, micro step. Whether it is reading more about an industry or field outside of your sport, learning and pursuing a new hobby, developing a new practice of meditation or breathing, finishing your degree, writing in a journal, growing your network, or whatever it may be, your actions need to be tiny. Every journey begins with a single step.

BJ Fogg, founder and director of the Behavior Design Lab at Stanford University, gives a framework on how to build new habits into our lives in his book, *Tiny Habits*. He emphasizes that it's not difficult to create new habits if you know what to look for and have a clear action plan. Fogg states, "The essence of *Tiny Habits* is this: Take a behavior you want, make it tiny, find where it fits naturally in your life, and nurture its growth. If you want to create long-term change, it's best to start small." When you look back at the various steps within the *SHIFT* framework, each movement forward, process, or progression begins with a simple step forward. Small moments create significant change and impact over time.

The simplicity of Fogg's work will help you break down how to create a new habit into your life. He intentionally keeps the process simple and tiny as well. He created his own version of the ABCs: anchor, behavior, celebration.[34]

Anchor Moment—An existing routine (like brushing your teeth) or an event that happens (like a phone ringing). The Anchor Moment reminds you to do the new Tiny Behavior.

New Tiny Behavior—A simple version of the new habit you want, such as flossing one tooth or doing two push-ups. You do the Tiny Behavior immediately after the Anchor Moment.

Instant Celebration—Something you do to create positive emotions, such as saying, "I did a good job!" You celebrate immediately after doing the new Tiny Behavior.

You desire to learn more about real estate or some other arena that could potentially become a focus of work after you are done playing. Each day after training, you take a nap. Your new habit could be something like this:

When you wake up from your nap, you go get a glass of water. You do two push-ups to get your blood flowing, pick up a book or article and read for five minutes, and then celebrate by pumping your fist into the air and saying, "good job."

It's a small, short, tiny new habit. Your anchor moment is waking up from a nap. Behavior is the new tiny habit of reading for five minutes. Then you have your celebration by pumping your fist in the air and telling yourself good job. These tasks are simple, tiny, and easy to introduce into your current life and rhythm with little to no reason to not begin establishing this new habit.

Take Action Today

What is one (or more) habit you desire to establish? What steps could you take by walking through Fogg's ABC's that you can establish today? Maybe it is building a consistent morning routine, thus setting yourself up for a successful day. Perhaps it's a desire to learn through reading more about a specific topic or new arena outside of sport, or to learn a new skill that will give you a leg up when you decide to make the transition to life after sport. Whatever the behavior may be, start simple and small by identifying those good habits you have and reinforcing them as well as identifying new habits you desire to develop to set you up to be successful.

Whether you are finishing your university career, still playing professionally, struggling through the transition post-playing, or already into your new career, what you do daily will guide you toward living your life at your best and successfully navigating the transitions that life and sport throw at you.

Working through what your ideal day and week look like will help guide and direct you toward your definition of success and what a successful life reflects. Examine your current actions and behaviors, being honest with yourself on what needs to change to see that ideal day and week come to fruition. Start small and look for those anchor moments and prompts or cues that kick-start your new behavior. What's interesting in sport is that you have created athletic habits that have benefited you well through the years, whether it is a cross-over in basketball, how you step onto the soccer field, or even how you put on your uniform, small behaviors that you do to prepare yourself for success. In this chapter, you are doing the exact same thing as you prepare for life after sport—creating good habits that prepare you to be at your best. You are created with purpose and intentionality, and it goes beyond what you can do in a race, on a field or court, or with a racket. Transitions are opportunities; leverage those opportunities for success and *Take Action*!

CONCLUSION

KEEP MOVING AND TAKE
THE NEXT BEST STEP

You don't have to see the whole staircase,
just take the first step.

—Martin Luther King Jr.

Life is more than a game, and so are you! When you
look at your life as an athlete, so much of it has been
focused on your sport. From when you wake up and
where you spend your time, what you focus on brings
you back to your sport and competition. At some point,
the competition will stop, and there will be no more
cheering fans, no more locker rooms, no more team
meals, practice sessions, ice baths—you get the idea.
It will all be over, but that doesn't mean your life is
over. Will you die twice? Once when you physically
die and once when you stop competing in your sport? I
don't know the answer to that question, but I do know

you will experience some form of grief when you stop competing. It's natural to have a sense of loss when you stop playing. You have given so much to your sport, and now it is gone. The important thing to remember is that your life is not over!

Your life has more to offer and give to this world than what you contributed to your sport and athletic performance. My hope and desire are that through this book and the *SHIFT* framework, you began to see yourself through a new lens. I want you to know that you truly are more than an athlete, greater than your numbers, and more significant than what you own or the trophies you have won. *Start Now*: Understanding who you are, your identity, and the power of your story and experience. *Heart*: How your values play a vital role in determining your behaviors and how life themes are guardrails for maximizing your strengths, skill sets, and discovering your why. *Imagine the Future*: Dream and think about what the future may hold, visualizing what could be on the horizon of your next step in life. Know what success looks like for you and where you are going as you find success. *Focus*: You control what you control, don't give your power away to others and be confident to say *No* to something to say *Yes* to what's best for you and the SMART goals you are tackling. *Take Action*: Eliminate the limiting beliefs you have bought into, learn how to create new good habits, and take ownership, be accountable, and take personal responsibility for yourself.

Playing the Long Game

Life is greater than any one moment or experience, even though it is difficult to see beyond those moments.

When you focus on living out your life in light of progression and development that never ends, you never stop pursuing growth. If each new day builds upon itself to make the most of the moments, and you believe each moment is building something special and unique, then the joy of the moment and growth never ends. Each moment in time is like a piece to a puzzle, and each day you have the opportunity to add to that puzzle something beautiful that will at the end of your life reveal something amazing.

As an elite athlete, you have a shelf life. I know it is hard to acknowledge that reality, but at some point, your athletic career will come to an end. Eventually, you will no longer be physically able to perform at your peak levels, your body will break down, and the sport industry will declare you not fit to compete. It is a harsh reality because you have given so much of your life to the game, but the forward movement for you and your life is not over. Every transition gives you an opportunity to grow, learn, develop, and build upon the previous arenas and transitions. The more you prepare for when that transition comes, the healthier and more successful you will be in and after that transition. It will still be difficult, and there will be struggles, but that is part of the process and life.

All of your hard work, focus, tenacity, sacrifice, success, experience, and relationships developed are not wasted once you are retired and move onto your next phase of life. Use your experience, leadership, character skills, and personal development as a stepping stone, building upon it as you move into your next arena. When you truly understand who you are and what and from where your value is derived, you will see your time as an elite athlete as a springboard to what's next. Is it difficult to stop competing? Yes, but it is not the end of the world or your life. You will grieve at some point, but you don't have to die as you continue to live.

Commit to SHIFT

One final word of encouragement: Life is bigger than your sport, and so are you. Your value and significance go beyond your stats, the wins and losses, your contract size, and the championships you have or have not won. My hope is you have learned this about yourself and know your life is significant. Your impact

Life is bigger than your sport, and so are you.

can go beyond your athletic career and affect the lives of those around you. Using your experience, athletic success, and development as a stepping stone will give you the courage to be your best self and positively impact the world around you. You may not change the world, but you can change your world for the better.

Legendary Green Bay Packers football coach Vince Lombardi said, "A man can be as great as he wants to be. If you believe in yourself and have the courage, the determination, the dedication, the competitive drive, and if you are willing to sacrifice the little things in life and pay the price for the things that are worthwhile, it can be done." Moreover, "Once a man has made a commitment to a way of life, he put the greatest strength in the world behind him. It's something we call heart power. Once a man has made this commitment, nothing will stop him short of success." Succinctly, he concluded, "The harder you work, the harder it is to surrender."

That is true for you and your life in sport, and more importantly, in life beyond your sport. Transitions and change can be difficult and tumultuous, but they can also provide significant opportunities. It is all about knowing yourself, having a clear perspective, being prepared, and having the courage and heart to keep going. Now is the time to maximize your *SHIFT*!

ACKNOWLEDGMENTS

I am forever grateful for the investment and opportunity my family has given me to pursue and explore writing and getting the ideas, thoughts, and perspective on paper. Rachel, you challenge, encourage, and push me to be a better version of myself every day. Thank you for loving me well through the valleys and over the mountain tops!

APPENDICES

Personal Value System Exercise:

Values reflect the things that matter the most to us; they are at the core of who we are and why we do what we do. When we live our best and most authentic life, it is usually lived through the filter of our values. Values are an important part of the decision process and define who we are as people. We don't always know or understand what they are or how they drive our lives.

List several characteristics of when you were at your best self. When you are living out your best true self, you are living out of your values.

If you were passing on a list of the top ten values required for a successful and full life for the next generation to read, what would they include?

Look over the list of values. Pick your top ten, then pick top five, four, three, two, and finally your top value.

This exercise helps to:

- Identify what your value system consists of, and gives boundaries and direction for your next steps
- Understand what you value, what is significant to you, and why
- Give clarity to your core and key motivations

Accountability	Creativity	Humility
Achievement	Curiosity	Humor
Adaptability	Decisiveness	Imagination
Adventure	Dependability	Influence
Affection	Determination	Innovation
Ambition	Diligence	Inspiration
Appreciation	Discipline	Integrity
Approachability	Diversity	Intelligence
Artistry	Education	Intimacy
Attentiveness	Effectiveness	Joy
Attitude	Empathy	Justice
Availability	Encouragement	Knowledge
Awareness	Endurance	Leadership
Balance	Enjoyment	Learning
Beauty	Excellence	Love
Belonging	Fairness	Loyalty
Boldness	Faith	Marriage
Bravery	Family	Mastery
Challenge	Financial	Maturity
Clarity	Independence	Meaning
Comfort	Flexibility	Mindfulness
Commitment	Focus	Motivation
Community	Freedom	Obedience
Compassion	Friendship	Open-mindedness
Competence	Frugality	Patience
Competition	Fun	Passion
Composure	Generosity	Peace
Confidence	Grace	Perseverance
Connection	Gratitude	Persistence
Consistency	Growth	Power
Contentment	Happiness	Preparedness
Control	Holiness	Proactivity
Conviction	Honesty	Professionalism
Cooperation	Honor	Prosperity
Courage	Hospitality	Purity

Rationality   Selflessness   Sympathy
Realism   Self-reliance   Teaching
Reason   Self-respect   Teamwork
Relaxation   Service   Thankfulness
Reliability   Significance   Trust
Resilience   Simplicity   Truth
Respect   Solitude   Understanding
Responsibility   Spirituality   Unity
Rest   Spontaneity   Vision
Sacrifice   Stability   Winning
Security   Strength
Self-control   Success

After identifying your top values, answer the following questions to help bring understanding and clarity to your values.

1. Why are these values most important to you?

2. Share a moment in your life when you were living out these values. What actions did you display that validated this value(s)?

3. How do you react when this value is not honored by those around you? What do you feel, what's your thought process or self-talk, actions?

4. Are you following these values in your life now? Give examples.

5. When you take a look at your daily and weekly actions and priorities, how do they reflect or conflict with your values? What is one change you need to make to move toward living your life through the filter of your values?

6. How does clarifying your values change some of your priorities related to work, family, friends, and faith?

Transferable Skills learned and developed as an athlete:

Key Skills:	Business Skills:	People Skills:
Meet Deadlines	Ability to Delegate	Build Trust
Results Oriented	Customer Service Oriented	Manage People
Organize and Plan	Increase Sales	Organize People
Accept Responsibility	Social Media	Delegate
Instruct Others	Marketing	Trust Others
Desire to Learn & Improve	Manage Projects	Teamwork
Time Management	Creative Thinking	Written Communication
Solve Problems	Analyze Information	Verbal Communication
Manage Money & Budgets	Compile Information	Body Language
Manage Projects	Research	Motivate Others
Critical Thinking	Take Inventory	Inspire Others
Independent Working	Design	Lead People & Projects
Computer Skills	Quality Control	Patient
Self-Motivated	Negotiate	Compassionate
Take Risks	Sales	Emotional Intelligence
Detail Oriented	Manage Meetings	Persuasive
Big Picture Thinking	Get Results	Challenge People
High Energy	Investigate	Coach and Mentor
Decisive	Teach and Train	Follow Instructions
Adaptable, Flexible	Public Relations	Listen
Outgoing		Support Other

ABOUT THE AUTHOR

Jonathan Van Horn enjoyed a successful athletic career but struggled with value, significance, and his identity as he made the transition to life after sport. During the past twenty years, Jonathan has journeyed alongside and mentored hundreds of university and professional athletes as they navigated various significant transitions: retirement, graduation, career-ending injuries, trades and off-seasons. Jonathan equips athletes to be and live at their best on and off the field of competition.

Jonathan writes on various topics related to leadership, character development, integration of faith and sport, and navigating transition. He continues to mentor current and retired pro athletes and assists coaches through developing character and leadership practices within their team cultures. Jonathan lives in North Carolina with his wife, Rachel, and three children Nora, Ellery, and Clara.

Connect at jonathanvanhorn.com

BIBLIOGRAPHY

1   "Football Transfers, Rumours, Market Values and News." *Transfermarkt*. www.transfermarkt.us.

2   Wooden, Andrew. "How Big Data Can Boost Athletic Performance." *Intel*. Accessed May, 19, 2020. www. intel.co.uk/content/www/uk/en/it-management/cloud-analytic-hub/big-data-powers-athletes.html.

3   *Lost Treasures of Egypt*. Documentary. 2019. UK: Windfall Films, 2019. TV Series. https://www.disneyplus.com/series/lost-treasures-of-egypt/5NZnohgMA1qa - accessed 4/13/2021

4   Proverbs 4:23, ESV.

5   "The Importance of the 88 Constellations." *Star Name Registry*, October 8, 2019, star-name-registry.org/blog/item/the-importance-of-the-76-constellations#:~:text=Constellations%20are%20useful%20because%20they,plant%20crops%20and%20harvest%20them.

6   Andrews, Andy. "How to Write a Personal Mission Statement by Answering 5 Questions."

Andy Andrews. www.andyandrews.com/personal-mission-statement/.

7   Proverbs 29:18, KJV.

8   Associated Press. "U.S. 400-meter relay teams doomed by flubbed handoffs, fail to qualify." *ESPN.* August 21, 2008. https://www.espn.com/olympics/summer08/trackandfield/news/story?id=3545991

9   Maddireddy, Mihir. "The Fastest Pit Crew You May Ever See Set a New World Record of 1.82 Seconds." *Car and Driver.* Nov. 18, 2019. www.caranddriver.com/news/a28567721/fastest-pit-stop-german-grand-prix/.

10 "How much communication is nonverbal" *Google Search.* Accessed May 10, 2020. www.google.com/search?q=how%2Bmuch%2Bcommunication%2Bis%2Bnonverbal&rlz=1C5CHFA_enUS810US810&oq=how%2Bmuch%2Bcommunication%2Bis%2B&aqs=chrome.0.0j69i-57j0l6.3909j0j7&sourceid=chrome&ie=UTF-8.

11 Lencioni, Patrick. *The Ideal Team Player: How to Recognize and Cultivate the Three Essential Virtues: a Leadership Fable.* Wiley India: Jossey-Bass, 2018.

12 Covey, Dr. Stephen R. "Habit 2: Begin With End In Mind." *FranklinCovey.* Accessed August 7, 2020. www.franklincovey.com/the-7-habits/habit-2.html.

13 Charles Swindoll. First heard this quote or variations of it from author and pastor Charles Swindoll.

14 Murphy, Austin. "A Lamb Among Lions" *SI.com Sports Illustrated Vault* Sept. 10, 1990. vault.si.com/vault/1990/09/10/a-lamb-among-lions-a-gentle-soul-off-the-field-barry-sanders-runs-up-a-storm-for-detroit.

15 Mathews, Ian. "No One Agreed With Barry Sanders Decision To Retire And 20 Years Later, He Has

No Regrets." *Forbes*. Accessed Sept. 13, 2019.
www.forbes.com/sites/ianmathews/2019/07/25/
no-one-agreed-with-barry-sanders-decision-to-
retire-and-20-years-later-he-has-no-regrets/
#748ac0a0415e.

[16] Press, Associated. "New book details Barry's reasons
for quitting." *ESPN*. Nov. 15, 2003. www.espn.com/
nfl/news/story?id=1662343.

[17] Dweck, Carol S. *Mindset: The New Psychology of
Success*. New York: Ballantine Books, 2008.

[18] Wooden, John. "The difference between winning and
succeeding." *TED*. Feb. 2001. www.ted.com/talks/
john_wooden_the_difference_between_winning_
and_succeeding?referrer=playlist-what_is_success.

[19] Accessed August 2020. I read and researched what is
success and the multiple definitions one could find
online, and here are four websites that helped shape
and guide these questions. All Accessed August
2020.

https://www.success.com/4-questions-i-asked-
myself-to-define-success/

https://www.prolificliving.com/define-success-10-
questions/

https://www.lifehack.org/articles/communication/
the-new-definitions-success.html

https://www.forbes.com/sites/amymorin/
2016/04/30/the-answer-to-this-question-wil
l-create-your-personal-definition-of-success/
#3af2454e101d

[20] Underdown, Jim. "Power Balance Bracelets
a Bust in Tests." *Skeptical Inquirer*. Jan. 2012.
skepticalinquirer.org/2012/01/power-balance-
bracelets-a-bust-in-tests/.

21   MacMahon, Tim. "Mark Cuban rips NBA over bracelets." *ESPN.* Nov. 26, 2012. www. espn.com/dallas/nba/story/_/id/8677068/ mark-cuban-dallas-mavericks-blasts-nba-scam-bracelet-deal.

22   "Abomination." *Dictionary.com.* www.dictionary. com/browse/abomination.

23   Yost, Missy. "19 Definitions Of Success You Should Never Ignore." *Lifehack.* Dec. 4, 2020. www.lifehack.org/articles/communication/ the-new-definitions-success.html.

24   Sandler, Seth. "NFL, MLB, NHL, MLS & NBA: Which Leagues and Players Make the Most Money?" *Bleacher Report.* March 18, 2012. bleacherreport. com/articles/1109952-nfl-mlb-nhl-mls-nba-which -leagues-and-players-make-the-most-money.

25   Brown, Daniel James. *The Boys in the Boat: Nine Americans and Their Epic Quest for Gold at the 1936 Berlin Olympics.* New York: Penguin, 2016.

26   "Oar." *Dictionary.com,* Dictionary.com, www.dictio-nary.com/browse/oar.

27   Dweck, Carol. "The power of believing that you can improve." *TED.* Nov. 2014. www.ted.com/talks/ carol_dweck_the_power_of_believing_that_you_ can_improve?language=en.

28   Whitbourne, Susan Krauss. "5 Reasons We Play the Blame Game." *Psychology Today.* Sept. 19, 2015. www. psychologytoday.com/us/blog/fulfillment-any-age/ 201509/5-reasons-we-play-the-blame-game.

29   Morin, Amy. "3 Types of Self-Limiting Beliefs That Will Keep You Stuck in Life (and What to Do About Them)." *Inc.* Sept. 14, 2018. www.inc.com/amy-mori

n/3-types-of-unhealthy-beliefs-that-will-drain-yo
ur-mental-strength-make-you-less-effective.html.

[30] Oppland, Mike. "How Psychology Combats False and Self-Limiting Beliefs." *PositivePsychology.com.* Sept. 1 2020. positivepsychology.com/false-beliefs/

[31] Berman, Robby. "New study suggests we have 6,200 thoughts every day." *Big Think.* July 16, 2020. bigthink. com/mind-brain/how-many-thoughts-per-day?re-belltitem=1#rebelltitem1.

[32] Michael Hyatt. I first heard this idea from Michael Hyatt on his blog—michaelhyatt.com—and *Best Year Ever* course; and have since heard multiple business leaders, leadership experts, and speakers share about the idea of a *messy middle.*

[33] Society for Personality and Social Psychology. "How we form habits, change existing ones." *ScienceDaily.* August 8, 2014. www.sciencedaily. com/releases/2014/08/140808111931.htm.

[34] Fogg, BJ. *Tiny Habits: The Small Changes That Change Everything.* Boston: Houghton Mifflin Harcourt, 2020.

*You've read **SHIFT**.*
Now it's time to take the online course.

THE

COURSE

Learn More
TheSHIFTCourse.com